We appli[...]
Bro. B[...]

Janell Richter

Jewels of Jude

BIBLE DEVOTIONAL

Carol Janell Johnston Richter

WestBow
PRESS®
A DIVISION OF THOMAS NELSON
& ZONDERVAN

Copyright © 2023 Carol Janell Johnston Richter.

All rights reserved. No part of this book may be used or reproduced by any means, graphic, electronic, or mechanical, including photocopying, recording, taping or by any information storage retrieval system without the written permission of the author except in the case of brief quotations embodied in critical articles and reviews.

This book is a work of non-fiction. Unless otherwise noted, the author and the publisher make no explicit guarantees as to the accuracy of the information contained in this book and in some cases, names of people and places have been altered to protect their privacy.

WestBow Press books may be ordered through booksellers or by contacting:

WestBow Press
A Division of Thomas Nelson & Zondervan
1663 Liberty Drive
Bloomington, IN 47403
www.westbowpress.com
844-714-3454

Because of the dynamic nature of the Internet, any web addresses or links contained in this book may have changed since publication and may no longer be valid. The views expressed in this work are solely those of the author and do not necessarily reflect the views of the publisher, and the publisher hereby disclaims any responsibility for them.

Any people depicted in stock imagery provided by Getty Images are models, and such images are being used for illustrative purposes only.
Certain stock imagery © Getty Images.

Scriptures are taken from King James version of the Bible, public domain.

Scriptures are taken from the New King James Version. Copyright © 1982 by Thomas Nelson, Inc. Used by permission. All rights reserved.

Scriptures are taken from the Holy Bible, New Living Translation, copyright © 1996, 2004, 2015 by Tyndale House Foundation. Used by permission of Tyndale House Publishers Inc., Carol Stream, Illinois 60188. All rights reserved.

Scriptures are taken from the Holy Bible, New International Version®. NIV®. Copyright © 1973, 1978, 1984 by International Bible Society. Used by permission of Zondervan. All rights reserved.

ISBN: 978-1-6642-9589-6 (sc)
ISBN: 978-1-6642-9590-2 (e)

Library of Congress Control Number: 2023905405

Print information available on the last page.

WestBow Press rev. date: 03/27/2023

Foreword

The Book of Jude is seldom quoted. There are few outstanding promises in the book of Jude; yet this half-brother of Christ has something to say to our twenty-first century Christians. The two basic themes are very relevant today. Theme One is "Stay Faithful to Truth." Theme Two is "Beware Deception."

May the God of all grace give us understanding and insight as we read.

Day One

JUDE VS. 3

CONTEND!

"Beloved, when I gave all diligence to write unto you of the common salvation, it was needful for me to write unto you, and exhort you that ye should earnestly contend for the faith which was once delivered unto the saints."

It seems that Jude had a desire to write to the Christian family, whom he called "Beloved." He wanted to write concerning the very positive theme of salvation; but before he could get his letter written, another more pressing issue arose. The brothers were experiencing a "faith attack."

Often when faced with extreme difficulties, fear will create doubts. Whereas, as long as all the bills are paid, we have extra money to jingle in our pockets, no one is upset at us, the children are all healthy, our plans are working out to suit us - we feel confident that we are pleasing God and nothing can go wrong!

On the other hand, just let the doctor tell us the spouse has cancer, the position we thought was secure is snatched from us, our home is about to be foreclosed, the car repossessed – then, we begin to question what we thought we believed, what we just knew to be true. It is at times like these that we need Jude to exhort us, to remind us, even to command us, "Contend."

What does "contend" mean? In the verse referenced, it means "To strive, to fight, to compete, to put forth effort." Wait! That sounds suspiciously like work! It is often exhausting to "contend." Sometimes victory seems unattainable. It can seem so far down the road, we grow weak trying to attain it.

Thank God, our whole life is not consumed with contending! Sometimes God gives us periods of rest. We can just float downstream looking with awe and appreciation at the canopy of trees overhead, giving us shade and amazing patterns of light and shadow. Life is effortless, during these times of rest. We feel sure we are going to arrive at the proper destination with little or no effort. Just sit back and relax.

In North Georgia at a little town called Helen, several companies provide tubing on the Chattahoochee River. It is nothing but a creek at this point. It meanders through the town of Helen, bubbling over several little waterfalls. One can rent a tube and sit back, letting the current take you through town. At the end of the trip there is someone to stop your tube, get you to shore, and motor you back to the starting point. All you have to do is stay on the tube and enjoy the sights along the way. You travel effortlessly.

Sometimes life is that easy. Enjoy those easy times. Thoroughly relish them! They will NOT last! Praise God for the time of rest, the time of ease, the time of quiet, because the roar of waterfalls is in the near future. Just around the next bend we will have white water to navigate. Is it a fearful experience? Oh, yes, but you will learn to "contend." You will learn how to thrust in the oar, how to evade the rocks. You will learn that every waterfall conquered, brings its own thrill! Without a test, there is no testimony! Without resistance there are no muscles built! Let us contend!

PRAYER: Father, thank you for the easy times of life. I've thoroughly enjoyed BOTH of them! (Smile) However, I know

You want us to become Mighty Warriors. We can't become strong without workouts. Recently, You have given me a difficulty to work through. I must contend, fight, put forth effort; but You will not leave me alone. You are right there beside me. Should this trial ever become more than my spiritual muscles can endure, You will come to my aid. Thank You for that assurance. Now, help me to contend for the faith, to wrestle with the angel, to fight the good fight – until YOU say it is enough. Amen.

Day Two

VS. 3

CONTEND? HOW?

Jude 3…..**earnestly** contend ….
Earnestly – with sincere and intense conviction

Some things are worth fighting for. Most things we value, we have struggled to obtain. We have fought to secure. There is a reason something is highly valued. Probably, because it cost us dearly! If it costs us nothing, we don't value it. If it costs us nothing, we don't treasure it.

When Jude commands us to "**earnestly** contend for the faith," he encourages us to put heart into our efforts. Have you ever pondered the scripture, Deut. 11:13-14, "If ye shall hearken diligently…..to love the Lord…..to serve Him with all your heart and with all your soul; then I will give you….."? The blessings came as a result of loving and serving with all that is in us.

A high schooler was attempting to impress on the coach that he was the one to represent the school in the "high jump" event in the district competition. The coach watched as the young man approached the bars, leaped, pushed and cleared the bar. "Yes, Son. That is very good; however, you will need to clear at least two feet higher to have any hope of being the champion. Let's raise the bar." The bar was raised and the student ran and jumped again and again, never quite clearing the mark. In sorrow, he picked himself up out of the landing pit and walked slowly away, his head hanging. "Wait, son," called his coach, running to catch up. "Let me make a suggestion." Putting his arm around the student's shoulders, he said, "Son, just get your heart over that bar. The rest of your body will follow!"

Our heart's desire will usually determine what we will pursue and how diligently we will work at it. We will put extreme effort into something we really desire. We will concentrate on it. We will make sacrifices for our heart's desire. Jesus acknowledged the power of the heart's desire when He said, "What things soever ye **desire**, when ye pray, believe that ye receive them, and ye shall have them." Mark 11:24. The key to receiving revealed in this verse, included not only believing, but also desire. That desire will have you praying, again and again. That desire will have you thinking about, working toward, confessing, believing for the desired result.

This race we are running, this battle we are fighting, will cost us something. It has cost some their lives. It will cost you. Jesus said, "If any man will come after me, let him deny himself, and take up his cross, and follow me." Matt. 16:24. This cross is not a pretty ornament. It is an instrument of death, specifically the death to self, to self-will. To follow through will require "heart….miles and miles of heart!" (Smile)

Putting all of life's distractions behind us, let us **earnestly** fight the good fight, **earnestly** run the race, **earnestly** contend for the faith. Let's put our heart into our running, with our whole heart serving and loving the Lord.

PRAYER: Father, help me to guard my heart so that the desires of this heart are only those that please you. Let me be earnest in my desire to please you. Help me to diligently serve You. Help me to put my whole heart into following You. The benefits to that kind of life are recorded both in Your Book and in history. Father, I am convinced. I surrender to Your way. My heart is Yours, my life is Yours, my all is Yours. Amen.

Day Three

JUDE, VS. 3

CONTEND? FOR WHAT?

Since "contending", fighting, resisting, putting forth effort is not necessarily fun, we need some definite reason for going to the effort. Right? Remember, when something is valuable, when something is precious to us, we find the strength needed to gain it and then to protect it.

Jude knows why THE FAITH is valued. Jude sees THE FAITH as truth that is definite, unchanging, and unchangeable. THE FAITH is truth that will set you free. THE FAITH is the revelation of Jesus who said, "I am the Way, the Truth and the Life…" John 14:6. THE FAITH is the solid Rock on which you can establish your life, plan your future, and depend on being the same yesterday, today, and forever. When the storms blow, it is the Rock which stands, unshaken.

How can you know if what you believe is THE FAITH ? How can you be assured that it is unchanging and unchangeable Truth, the Word of God? Many people have questioned, many have doubted. They call themselves agnostics or atheists. By the way, did you know we have one holiday, annually, for atheists? Oh, yes, it is April 1, April Fools day. (The fool hath said in his heart there is no god! Smile, it won't hurt you!)

Pilot, at the trial of Christ said, "What is truth?" John 18:38. The records do not show whether he ever found truth, but other doubters have. C.S. Lewis started out to prove that Christianity was not true and as a result of his research found the One who said, "I am the Way, the Truth and the Life." He wrote many books about his search including Tales of Narnia for children (of all ages!)

Lee Stroebel decided as a college student that he was an atheist. He married a girl who agreed that she too was an atheist. Then, she found The Way, The Truth and The Life! In anger, Lee decided to prove to her that there was nothing to God, nothing to the Bible. Using his experience as an investigative reporter, he diligently followed every lead, chased every clue. He finally realized that if he were going to be intellectually honest, he had to admit, Jesus is The Truth, The Way, The Life! From his experiences came the book The Case For Christ!

If you "earnestly contend for the faith," you will eventually be convinced of its truth and of its value. If you are not yet convinced of the truth of the Bible, of the existence of Almighty God, of the Sonship of Jesus, of the power of the Holy Spirit, you must start there. You can read the works of others who have been convinced. The two authors mentioned above will be helpful.

Another way to discern "Truth" is to ask yourself, "Is this fact true in all generations? Is this true in all cultures?" Sometimes we have to admit that some of our favorite little ideas are just that – OUR ideas. They have to do with our preferences not with God's truth. The FAITH is truth God reveals to humans about Himself, His character, His purpose.

Another valuable consideration in deciding what is true is to compare what you believe to the creation. "The heavens declare the glory of God; the firmament shows His handiwork." Ps.19:1. We can readily observe the following facts about the creation: its vast variety, its bounteous beauty, its outstanding order! The creation is ruled by faithful, dependable laws. You can jump off the roof anywhere in the world and you will fall DOWN. You can depend on that! The Law of Gravity will take you down!

You can also depend on the sun rising, the tides rising and falling. It is true on any continent, during any season. Those natural laws are the same. The planets and the stars will stay in their orbits and appear again at the proper times. That law is so consistent, we can go to the future and predict where in our solar system the planets will be at any given time, or where in their orbits a specific star will be. The FAITH is just as dependable.

Compare what you believe to the Jesus of the Bible. He is the express image of the Father; He will show you the Father. He is the same yesterday, today and forever. His purpose is the same….to seek and to save the lost. His character is the same……revealing the Father to mere mortals. His Words, His actions are what He has seen and heard from the Father. In history, everywhere Jesus was made the central focus of life, **good** was the result.

Does it really matter what you believe? Yes, because what you believe, directs your actions. If I believe the house is on fire, I run out. My safety, perhaps my life, depends on my knowing and believing the truth.

PRAYER: Heavenly Father, when I see the Heavens, the work of Your hands, and all You have made, I wonder, "What is man that You are mindful of him, the son of man that You deign to visit him." May I please see clearly the path before me. For if I can see clearly, if I can discern truth from error, I won't stumble in the darkness of my doubts into error. May I find my place in You and be content to stay there! May I see clearly Your plan for me and step by step follow You from glory to glory.

Day Four

JUDE VS. 3

WHAT IS WORTH FIGHTING FOR?

Vs. 3 " Beloved, when I gave all diligence to write unto you of the common salvation, it was needful for me to write unto you, and exhort you that ye should earnestly contend for the faith which was once delivered unto the saints."

Jude under the inspiration of the Holy Ghost urges us to Contend for the faith. Not everything is worth our putting up a fight. One very wise man said, "Choose your battles." If you become upset about everything, if you struggle over every decision, if you are constantly contending, you will soon become worn to a frazzle as the old folks say.

Nevertheless, there are some things that are worth fighting for. One is our "faith" - our grasp of the truth, our understanding of God's plan for us. When we have an attack on our faith, when our enemy tries to make us doubt God's love and concern for us, it is time to contend, time to resist.

This particular doubt, that God does not have our best interest at heart, that God does not love us, why, that's the same doubt that Lucifer presented to Eve in the garden.

"God knows that if you eat of that fruit you will become even as the gods." Gen. 3:5. And that enemy, the devil, convinced Eve to doubt God's love and care, even suggesting that God does not want us to be like Him. Well, that is definitely a lie! God **does** have a plan for us to become like Christ, but through **His** plan and by **His** power. Remember the verse, "…when he shall appear, we shall be like him, for we shall see him as he is…" I John 3:2.

The faith, the body of truth by which we live is so important to our well-being here in this natural life, and "the faith" certainly determines where we spend our eternal future. We must contend with any and every enemy that hinders our living by that faith. "The just shall live by faith.!" Hab. 2:4 (and 3 other places in the Bible) "He that believeth….hath an everlasting life."

Contending for THE FAITH, sometimes means resisting the popular thought of the times.

Sometimes contending for the faith means applying God's Word to our decisions rather than human reasoning.

Sometimes contending for the faith means struggling with outward physical evidence. We are spiritual creatures in a hostile physical environment. Our spiritual senses tell us God is truth and that He is always right, despite what we feel or hear or see. But what we sense with the natural senses holds a powerful influence over us. To go against those senses, takes tremendous trust and powerful faith in God. Now we can understand why we must "contend" for it.

There are at least three types of Faith mentioned in scripture: (1.) The gift of faith, one of the nine gifts of the spirit, I Cor. 12:9; (2.) The measure of faith given to everyone in order to be saved, Rom. 12:3; and (3.) The fruit of faith listed in Gal. 5:22. We can understand that a gift is handed to us, totally unearned, just given. We also understand that fruit growing takes time, and cultivating fruit takes effort. This must be that faith spoken of when the book says, "Faith cometh by hearing and hearing by the Word of God."

I once ask a preacher, one in whose life I had seen miracles, as well as Godly character, "How do you know when it is God speaking to you? How can you be so sure you are being directed by the Spirit and not just by your own desires?" His answer so astonished me, I have been considering it for years. (II Tim. 2:7).

He said, "You learn to know the voice of God by trial and error. If there is no check in your spirit, if you continue to have peace about a decision, you move boldly in that direction. Then watch for the results, the fruit. If the fruit are Godly, you will heed that voice the next time you hear it. Likewise, if things don't turn out in a Godly manner, you will be very cautious of that voice next time you hear it."

In trying to apply the preacher's suggestion in my life, I recalled how Jesus said, "My sheep know my voice." Sheep, not lambs. The sheep have learned to know and follow the shepherd's voice. The lambs just follow the ewe.

Being faithful to follow the truth entrusted to us through both the written Word and the living Word, brings us to eternal life through Jesus Christ.

PRAYER: Father, please help me to be discerning. May I know Your voice and discern Your truth and fight to cling to that truth which is called The Faith. If there's anything worth fighting for, it must certainly be the Truth. That same Truth, who said, "I am the Way, the Truth, and the Life", Jesus. May I be more like You each day. Amen.

Day Five

JUDE, VS. 3

THE FAITH.

Vs. 3. "Beloved, when I gave all diligence to write unto you of the common salvation, it was needful for me to write unto you, and exhort you that ye should earnestly contend for the faith…"

The Faith, the body of Truth recorded in the Bible and proven over the centuries, is a firm foundation on which to build our lives. Jesus said it this way, "whoever hears these sayings of Mine, and does them, I will liken him to a wise man who built his house on the rock." Matt. 7:24. You remember the story, how the winds came and the rains fell and beat upon the house, but it stood firm. The Truth will stand firm in times of storms.

Truth will stand inspection and come out clean and victorious. Nitpicking is a great pass time for persons who are still trying to find the truth through their own efforts. Others are trying to make Truth agree with their impression and understandings. Pastor Richter says, "If you are always splitting hairs over different understandings of the Bible, eventually all you will have is a hand full of hairs!" Just cast yourself on Jesus and ask Him to reveal His truth to you.

Have you been discouraged at some point because of the divisions and denominations in the Body of Christ, the Church? Most of these came about because of some difference in understanding some portion of scripture. Our loving and merciful Heavenly Father loves all of us and manages to use all of us in His Kingdom despite our lack of understanding. We may find out in the end that we are ALL mistaken about some scripture! Christ reminds us TO LOVE (John 15:12) and that LOVE WILL COVER A MULTITUDE OF SINS. James 5:20, I Peter 4:8.

Truth will stand the test of time. When further knowledge is uncovered, as in science, it always vindicates what God's truth has said all along. In ages gone by, scholars took the saying "four corners of the earth" to mean the earth was square. No doubt we should have understood it to mean, the four directions of the earth, north, south, east, west. In Isaiah 40:22, we read, "It is He who sits above the circle of the earth." In the pictures taken during man's space travel, we could see that the earth is round and could attest that Job 26:7 is true, "He hangs the earth upon nothing."

Man's understanding is so small compared to the knowledge and wisdom of our God, we learn quickly to depend on what God has said, rather than to be swayed by our senses or by what man is saying. Anyone who has ever attended a magic show can attest to how easily the human eye can be fooled and the human mind confused.

Deception is growing as the end of the age approaches. The very nature of deception is that it looks a lot like the true, the genuine. To be even the least bit deceiving there has to be an element of truth mingled with the error. How then are we to know the truth?

Salesmen sometimes comment with disdain, that women are more easily convinced than men. Others have pointed out that Christians are more easily fooled than the general populace. Perhaps it is good that the Church is trusting, expecting their associates to be truthful. Who would want a friend who is always skeptical, always finding something to doubt. The grace of God has given us a loving and trusting nature; however, the power of the Holy Spirit protects us, working in us to discern the truth. When we have determined to obey Jesus, we become like the WISE man, who built his house on the Rock.

"The Faith delivered the saints," based on the Holy Bible will stand. Jesus said it this way, "Heaven and earth will pass away, but my words shall not pass way." Matt. 24:35.

PRAYER: Dear Father, I determinedly cling to the truths you have revealed both in the Bible and through Jesus Christ, the living Word. I am basing all my decisions on these truths, believing Your promises, "He that believeth…..hath an everlasting life."

Day Six

JUDE, VS. 3

"THE FAITH ONCE DELIVERED THE SAINTS."

Sometimes when we say THE before a word, we mean the one and only, or the main one, or the important one. Jude decides to go a step further in specifying THE FAITH. He qualifies the term with the words "**once delivered the saints.**" God gave His revelation of Himself to His people, once and for all time. It is never changing; it never has to be updated. It is TRUTH for all time! OK, then why the difference in the God of the Old Testament and the Jesus of the New?

God **begins** revealing Himself to His people in the Old Testament. It is a frame by frame, picture by picture portraying of Himself. "Look, this is Who I AM," He says to Moses. Then, after centuries of showing Himself to Israel, finally, the greatest unveiling of Himself is in the person of Jesus Christ. Christ is the most complete revelation to humanity of who God is.

The God of the Old Testament is teaching young and inexperienced Children about Himself, His strength, His authority, His ways, and yes, at times, His mercy. But, in the New Testament, God, through Christ, shows His understanding of the human condition, His compassion for human inadequacies, His plan to reconcile mankind unto Himself, even calling him "Sons", Heirs of the Father, Joint-heirs with Christ. His relationship with us has changed because of Christ!

Apply this understanding to our childrearing. Early in our child's life, we establish who is boss, who has the authority, whose word must be obeyed. If we fail to do that early in the child's life, we often rear unruly, disobedient youths to whom the hard knocks of life must teach the lessons the child failed to learn earlier from loving and patient parents.

When I was rearing my children I read a book about childrearing which told the following story illustrating the importance of instant obedience. A family of three, father, mother and toddler, was taking a walk. The toddler ran ahead. Father with his eyes on his child, saw that they were approaching an intersection and that a car was speeding toward them on that intersecting road. The toddler, some twenty feet ahead, was in danger of stepping into the path of the car. Father screamed, "Stop," with all the urgency of a frightened parent! The well-trained child came to an immediate stop, the car rushed past and everyone was safe! Obedience to our Heavenly Father brings us just such safety and deliverance!

As our children become adults, our relationship with them changes. No longer are we required to make every decision, or to watch constantly over them, alert for danger. The child takes on more responsibility for his own welfare. We begin to relate more as friends, almost equals. Jesus pointed this out when he said to His disciples, "I'll call you no longer servants (who will be constantly told what to do), but friends (who know the heart and desires of their friend)." John 15:15.

This FAITH that has stood the test of time reveals our Heavenly Father as indeed faithful, loving, forgiving. AND He is Father who knows when to be strong, correcting, authoritative. Today, it seems we in ministry like to show **only** the merciful, tender side of Father. Yes, it is true that God is merciful, forgiving, showering humans with His grace, but there is the strong side of Father also. Read Ex. 34: 7. He will not excuse wrongdoing. His mercy does not excuse sin. This side of God is part of the FAITH, too. It is dangerous to forget that obedience is still demanded!

This Faith, once delivered the saints is the same Truth, the same God, the same Jesus, the same Way as revealed from the beginning. God is just too big to grasp in one session, one glimpse, one revelation. It's like looking at the huge globe of the earth. We stand looking at the Western Hemisphere, North and South America, and we say, "I know exactly what the earth looks like. There is a large land mass in the northern part of the globe and another land mass in the southern part of the globe. Both the east and west sides of the land masses are bordered by huge oceans."

But a person standing on the other side of the globe would say, "Oh, no. That is not the earth at all. There is a tremendous land mass on the north, (Asia) with a large island on the south (Australia) and two or three peninsulas of land jutting into the southern seas." Just about the time you feel you KNOW what the earth looks like, the globe turns and you see the earth from another viewpoint.

To see the whole nature of our wonderful, loving Father is to, on the one hand, rejoice in the truth of His tender love and mercy, **and** on the other hand, to expect strong discipline if we fail to do right. Yes, He is good and gentle, giving us a second chance and even third and fourth chances. **AND** He is too loving to allow us to follow the path that leads to destruction without firmly applying the rod of correction. God loves us *just like we are* **AND** He loves us too much to leave us just like we are!

PRAYER: FATHER, I have known You in good times and in bad times. I have learned to trust You even when things hurt and

Jewels of Jude

I don't understand Your purposes. I have learned You are faithful to Your children. Thank you for the mercy You show AND thank you for the stumbling blocks You are willing to put in our paths to keep us from racing headlong into destruction. You have caused us to understand, You are the same, yesterday, today and forever.

Day Seven

JUDE, VS. 4

CERTAIN MEN CREPT IN UNNOTICED

"For there are certain men crept in unawares…"

Because of the beautiful, trusting nature of the Family of God, we often need shepherds, Pastors, to guard us and warn us of ungodly men who creep in unnoticed. A person whose intentions are good and right need never go creeping slyly through the flock. They walk with openness and purpose. Good and Godly leaders have good and Godly purposes.

The New Testament urges us to "know those who labor among you." I Thess. 5:12. Perhaps it is a sincere desire to avoid "judging" that influences many Christians to ignore clear evidence that certain laborers are exhibiting behavior that is not becoming to Christians. We sometimes fail to be alert when wolves, dressed in sheep's clothing, creep in. It is not that we want to be suspecting and critical of everyone who comes to minister to us. Neither do we want to let evil men creep in unnoticed and hurt the trusting ones that God has put in our care.

How do we know who is godly and who is ungodly? The Bible tells us, "Ye shall know a tree by the fruit it bears." Matt. 7:16-17. If we see the fruit of the spirit, love, joy, peace, etc. (Gal. 5:22), in their lives, if their actions follow the pattern of the life of Christ, if the commandments of the Lord are honored and obeyed, then you know that person is godly.

Is it possible to be deceived? Even when looking at the fruit? Except for the power of the Holy Spirit, I suppose any of us could be; however, remember, we are Children of God. He is our shield, our Protector. He is the force who Sealed us with His Spirit,(Eph. 4:30). He reveals to the prophets the threats to His children, just as He did here in Jude, Vs. 4. Our part is to stay alert, to be watchful, to stay in tune with Jesus.

So, what are the dangers of which Jude warns us? The first is so prevalent today, one would think Jude is speaking to this generation. "God is so good, He won't punish anyone for immorality." "God's grace is so great, everything is forgiven. Live any way you want. You can't possibly be un-forgiven." "God wouldn't send anyone to hell. He's too good."

These men in Jude Vs. 4 are wrongly assuming that God's grace means "no moral laws." However, if you remember, when Jesus talked about the law in Matthew, Chapters 5-7, His understanding was tighter than the Old Testament view. "You have heard it said, 'Love your neighbor, hate your enemy.' I say, love your enemy." "You have heard, do not commit adultery. I say if you lust after a woman, you have committed adultery in your heart." "You have heard, do not kill, but I say if you are angry with your brother without provocation you are in danger of the judgment." Matt. 5.

The beautiful thing about being saved, having Jesus in your heart, is that the law of Christ is now in our hearts. We don't need an external law, "Thou shalt not kill." We don't WANT to kill! The "want- to" is taken out. Instead the LOVE of Christ is now in our hearts.

But the thing that frustrated the author is that the beautiful GRACE of God is used as an excuse for sin and that the very life and purpose of our Jesus Christ is denied.

You see, it is the GRACE of God and the person of Jesus Christ who left the 99 safe in the fold and went out of the safety, out into the storms of this life, out into the rough and dirty crags of this rocky world to look for that one lost, helpless sheep. That one lost sheep is you or me! Matt. 18:12.

PRAYER: Dear Shepherd, thank you for your willingness to seek and save that one lost sheep. Thank you that You were willing to leave the ninety and nine and seek till you found me. You placed strong and loving arms around me and brought me back to the safety of the fold. Help me to be alert to the deceptions of the enemy, to keep my eyes on You, to follow You, and to keep my ears attuned to Your voice. Amen

Day Eight

JUDE, VS. 4

BEWARE DECEPTION

The problem with deception is that it is deceiving! (Smile!) You know the saying, "If it sounds like a duck, if it looks like a duck, then it probably **is** a duck!" OK, unless it is a deception. Sometimes things look right, they sound right, but when compared to the truth, those things are just not right.

We have been to magic shows where things appear one way, but in reality are quite different! Remember how they put the girl into a wooden box with her head hanging out one end and what appears to be her feet hanging out the other. The magician takes a saw and goes to work, sawing in the middle of the box. At the end of the trick, the girl appears to be sawed completely into two parts. Then they show us how they did the trick! Aw, but it looked so real! That's why it is deceiving, because it looked real.

Generally, deception must have some kernel of truth or it is not believable. Consider the "Prosperity Doctrine", and I'm defining this doctrine as "unless you are financially well-off, you are not God's child, or you are not in His will." The Word tells us it is God's will for us to have plenty, enough and to share. Any parent wants his child to do well. Certainly, God wants His children to have plenty. Many scriptures tell us He will see that we have enough. Then where is the deception? We become children of God, not by amassing wealth, but by believing and confessing. Rom. 10: 9-10.

Deception is so cunning that we are frequently warned to beware. One example is the exhortation, "beware the leaven (doctrine) of the Pharisees." Mark 8:15. Man's thoughts are often twisted by what we consider pleasant, right, fair. **Be reminded** that the human heart is desperately wicked… **AND that** God's thoughts are high above ours and are always right and just. **AND that** there is a way that seems right to man, but the end thereof is the way of death.

Do you remember in Genesis 3, when the serpent questioned Eve concerning the intent of our Father? Besides lying, "Ye shall NOT die," he said, "God knows your eyes will be open and you will be like gods…" inferring that God is withholding from us something precious, that He doesn't want us to be like Him. (I'm not saying supernatural creatures. I'm saying like God in character and purpose.) The whole plan of Christ coming to redeem us, the Spirit's indwelling to form us into His character, is that we be like our Father!

Jesus came teaching us to call His Father, our Father. He said, "Look at me and you will see what our Father is like. Be like me and you will be like our Father. Be ye perfect even as your Father which is in heaven is perfect." Matt. 5:48, John 14:9-14.

Then we protest, "But Jesus, we are human. We can't do it. We can't live it. We can't be like you – perfect."

Not in ourselves, we can't. But God gave us two resources to help make it possible. The First is the Blood of the Lamb, by God's grace. Because of the shed blood of Jesus in which we are wrapped, covered over with His blood, God does not see our sins, but the blood sacrifice of His son, Jesus. God's grace, God's mercy, God's favor is bought with a dear price – the blood of Jesus.

The Second thing making it possible for us to live lives pleasing to God is the indwelling Holy Spirit, writing God's way, God's law, on the fleshly tables of our hearts. Acts 1:8, "Ye shall receive power after the Spirit is come upon you and ye shall be witnesses of me....." witnesses not with just words, but also in actions, life-style, in power. In other words, we look, act, talk so much like Christ we are called Christians!

PRAYER: Dear Jesus, live in me. Live the life of the Father through me, that I might be like You, a light in this dark world. Let me be preserving salt in the midst of this awful decay. Let the power of the Holy Spirit empower me to say "NO" to the forces of evil and darkness around me. Let me be alert, ever watchful for the enemy. My desire is to be Your Ambassador, Your Representative in my home, in my church, in my world. Amen.

Day Nine

JUDE, VS. 4

CERTAIN MEN, UNGODLY DECEIVERS

"For there are certain men crept in unawares, who were before of old ordained to this condemnation, ungodly men, turning the grace of our God into lasciviousness, and denying the only Lord God, and our Lord Jesus Christ."

We expect deceivers in the world. We expect deceivers to be in bad places doing their best to influence the children of this world to continue their ungodly ways, but in the church? We don't want to have to watch our backs at church! The most hurtful thing ever is to find someone we thought to be righteous and helpful, who turned out to be unrighteous, unholy, and deceitful. That's why we must "Know them that labor" (I Thess. 5:12) among us. By the Spirit!

What is the problem in this verse? These ungodly men are teaching that because God's grace covers us, we are free to participate in unlawful sensual pleasures in the body, licentiousness. You know the argument, "Where sin does abound, grace does much more abound." Rom. 5:20. Grace is good, right? The more sin the more grace, so let's sin a lot so we'll get a lot of grace. But wait! Yes, in Romans 5, Paul is encouraging us that no matter how great our sin, no matter how awful, God's grace is sufficient to cleanse it through the blood of Jesus; however, we don't HAVE to sin!

Three times in Romans 6, Paul says we are freed from the bondage or control of sin, vs. 7, vs. 18 and vs.22. How can this be? Aren't we still human? Don't we still have the capacity to sin? Afraid so! However, NOW that we are saved by the blood of Jesus, our desires are different. We desire to please Christ; therefore, we refuse to allow our body and mind to participate in activities that are unlike our blessed Savior, Jesus Christ.

Since I am FREE in Christ, can't I then do anything I want? No, not unless what **you** want is what **HE** wants. You see, He knows the end result of the licentious actions the body sometimes desires. He wants to deliver you from the death that follows these kinds of activities, so He frees you to make choices to do right!

I know a beautiful young woman who, as a teenager, was caught up in immoral activities that resulted in an illegitimate child. This child grew to be a brilliant young man with hope and a bright future ahead. Then he came under wrong influences and began to make some of the same choices his mother had made in her youth. I watched her grieve and try to redirect his paths. She knew exactly the hurt and heartache his choices would bring. Just so, our Jesus knows that "the wages of sin is death, but the gift of God is eternal life…"Rom. 6:23 And He has made a way for our escape!

The fourth verse of Jude continues to grieve, "and denying the only Lord God…" Not only does licentious living bring about death, this life-style denies the very character of our God who is holy and our Jesus Christ who came to make it possible for us to live holy lives through His shed blood and His indwelling Spirit.

It **is** possible for you to live a holy life! It **is** possible for you to be like Christ! Hey, I didn't say it was easy! (smile) Just, that it is possible! How? **Step One:** Grow! Eph. 2:21, Eph. 4:15; I Pet. 2:2; II

Pet. 3:18. You were BORN again, a babe in Christ; now you must grow up. Just eat and you will grow...eat the good Word of God. **Step Two:** Deal with sin, immediately. I John 1:9. Since you are a CHILD (of God), you will make mistakes, sins, errors. Deal with it. Confess it. Put it under the blood! Learn from it and grow! **Step Three:** Daily die to self. Put down self's will, self's desires and take up His desires for you. **Step Four:** Ask Father to fill you with His Holy Spirit. The Spirit will give you the POWER to live the Christ-life. The Spirit will produce the Fruit of the Spirit, Gal.5:22, in you. It is "Christ in you, the hope of glory!" Col. 1:27.

PRAYER: Dear Father, I see too much of me and too little of Jesus when I look at my life and activities. Please help me to follow Jesus so closely that I will begin to look like Him, to act like Him. Lord, I see that it is denying You, if I fail to reflect You to those around me. Finally, I see that You WANT me to be like You. Come, live inside of me. Make me more like You. Amen.

Day Ten

VS. 4

UNGODLY MEN CREPT IN

Jesus warned us to beware wolves who are dressed in sheep's clothing. In other words, they look right. But inwardly they are "ravening wolves," dangerous to the flock, especially the very young in the flock. We have heard complaints that we in the church are too "judgmental." No one wants our Godly leaders to be critical of everyone and everything that does not agree with their preferences. Certainly, we want to show mercy and grace as our Heavenly Father and our Lord Jesus does.

Neither do we want to hire the fox to guard the hen house! Why? It is the fox's nature to eat the hens. It is the enemy's nature to destroy the sheep of God. That's why we must be aware! Jesus said to WATCH and pray. To be aware that there are wolves masquerading as sheep in the sheep fold.

Whose responsibility is it to watch out for the wolves? Of course, the primary responsibility falls on the shoulders of the Shepherd of the Flock. However, as you mature in the Lord, your place will be to come alongside the Shepherd and to be aware of falsehoods and false people who would knowingly or even unknowingly destroy the flock.

In the area of finances, you wouldn't knowingly put your money in the hands of someone who has been deceptive in that area in the past. If greed and covetousness has been a weakness in the past, it may still be a weakness even though that person is sincerely trying to overcome the flesh and follow the Good Shepherd. You do him a disservice to put him in charge of money. That is a tempting position for him, and you bring the whole church under possibility of loss. It just isn't wise. Be Aware!

If there is someone in the Body of Believers who has in the past been accused of child molestation, you don't put them over your children's ministry. Yes, they may not even be guilty, or they may have repented and are growing in the Lord. However, if there is suspicion there, YOU be aware. If there is still a weakness there, you don't want to take part in putting a new convert in this tempting situation. You certainly don't want any lamb (child) wounded! Be Aware!

Guard your Shepherd! Guard those in leadership! The enemy of our soul loves to slay the Shepherd and scatter the sheep. Don't leave him alone with a member of the opposite sex even to "Help" that person. You stay in the vicinity so that there is a witness that no wrong was done. Be Aware!

OK. I can just hear our enemy, "You are going to become suspicious of everyone! You are always going to be watching your back!" No. What we are going to do is submit ourselves to the Lord, we are going to pray for a pure heart and a pure mind, AND we are going to be alert!

A Pastor near us was trying, to the best of his ability, to minister to a divorcee in his church. One night she called asking the pastor to come to her home. "I'm losing my mind," she screamed. "Please come and pray for me."

The pastor's spouse said, "I'm going with you."

"What about the children," he replied? "They are already asleep." The First Lady called a woman in the church to hurry over to stay with the children and the two travelled to the distraught woman's house.

When the woman came to the door she was clothed in nothing but a see-through negligee! She opened the door, throwing herself at the Pastor. That's when she saw he was accompanied by his wife. "Oh, look at me," she groaned, "See, I'm losing it!" It was amazing how fast she came to her senses! She went to put on something decent; the pastor and wife prayed and departed.

We will not let evil men (or women) creep into our sheep fold unawares, putting our little ones, our leaders, our ministries in danger. We WILL BE AWARE!

PRAYER: Father, guard our hearts that we not become harsh, judgmental, suspicious, critical, cynical. Neither let us be naïve, or unguarded. Help us to remember we have an Enemy. He is a sly old fox, conniving and deceitful and he doesn't care who he uses to destroy us. He hates us because we belong to You and he hates You. You have commanded us to love everyone, even our enemies, but you have not commanded us to trust anyone, but You. We are all flesh and subject to fail, but You are our Lord and our Savior. Our help comes from You. Help us to know Your voice and to follow close to You. The LORD is my Shepherd. Amen.

Day Eleven

VS. 4,

UNGODLY MEN TURNING GRACE INTO LASCIVIOUSNESS

How can something so pure, so clean, producing such good for all, GRACE, be turned into such filth, such self-serving actions? If you haven't already learned, human nature is certainly "I" centered and self-serving. It is HIS divine nature that we are seeking to take on, to live out through these fleshly temples.

What is GRACE? Grace is receiving good you don't deserve! To think on His grace, is to see HOPE in every direction. We humans are in the pit. We are hopelessly mired in a bog of filth. We can't possibly get out without help. We have struggled with the effort till we are exhausted, when along comes our Creator, whom we have rejected, whose ways we have despised, whose wisdom we have denied. He has a plan. He makes a way. He reaches way down and drags us out. He sets our feet on a solid rock. He washes us clean.

He makes us His child, His heir, and He begins to groom us to take our place in the kingdom!

What is lasciviousness? It is responding to the human sexual desire without regard for rules of behavior or laws of faithfulness to spouse. We call it licentious, unprincipled in sexual matters. These ungodly men, having crept into the flock, are now teaching the young ones, that God's grace will make allowances for unprincipled, unlawful, ungodly behavior.

Remember where God found us? We were captured, we were in chains, we were on the auction block in Satan's slave market, being auctioned cheaply to the thoughtless crowd. We were dirty, unkempt, nearly naked before the mocking throng, but our Jesus paid the ultimate price to buy us out of that slave market and off that auction block.

Then the GRACE of God, began the cleaning process. Washing the filth of this world off us, tending the wretchedness of broken nails, broken teeth, broken heart, clothing us in the purity and cleanliness of His person. But, that is not all. The GRACE of God, led us to Father's throne and offered us an honored position in the household, that of Child of the King, Father God.

The GRACE of God continued working with us in the re-training process, renewing our minds, so we could think like Father, Love like Father, Live like Father, Give like Father. No wonder Jude was so out-raged that anyone would use this wonderful GRACE as an excuse to jump back into the pit, get back into the same chains, smeared with the same filth, from which Jesus Christ had given His life, shed His blood to free us.

How can anyone who has been set free from the chains of the enemy, deny the saving, cleansing power of the blood of Jesus Christ? The very reason for the human life of Jesus Christ was His redemption of mankind. The suffering on the Cross was suffering He endured in our place. The stripes of the whip on His back were for our healing. The pierced hands, the pierced feet, the pierced side, the pierced brow, all poured the precious blood that purchased our freedom from the slave market of our enemy.

PRAYER: Thank you, Jesus, for your life, lived as a testimony to man of the kind of life Father wants us to live. Thank you for the model you gave us of love and compassion and giving. Thank you for showing us how it is done. Thank you for showing us how to have victory over sin, Satan, self. Thank you for showing us how to exercise authority in the spirit realm and in the natural realm.

Then, thank you, Jesus, for your death. In that death you became the sacrificial lamb, dying in my place. I deserved to die, but you took my place. I deserved the beating, but you took my place. I deserved the suffering, but you took my place. Oh, my Jesus. I can never deny You, or what You did on Calvary's cross. Amen and Amen." "Oh, the blood of Jesus....that washes white as snow."

Day Twelve

JUDE, VS 4

TURNING GRACE INTO LASCIVIOUSNESS

Another look at this idea! We have been captured by the enemy of our Father, the King! This enemy has stripped us of any vestige of our royal heritage. He has beaten us until we are bruised and bloody. Unkempt and unlovely we are placed on the auction block to sell to the highest bidder. Which addiction shall it be? Sex? Drugs? Alcohol? It seems our destiny is to be a slave! Then the troops of our Father rush in! The Holy Spirit is the Captain! The Church, the saints, the preachers, the leadership, are all there to help rescue us! We are snatched off the auction block and rushed to the safety of Father's house where the Holy Spirit begins to clean us up, to heal our wounds and to teach us Father's way. What fool would escape out the back door and go back to the slave market!?

These are pictures of Father's grace. To see us as worthy of the sacrifice of His Son, is mind boggling. Then to suggest that we can fulfill Father's dream for us while playing in the mire of the pit?

That we can be a slave to anything and at the same time a child of the King? That is ludicrous!

But the deceiving men were "turning God's grace into lasciviousness." What does lasciviousness even mean? If you want to take a glimpse into the meaning, look at Gal.5:19-21. "But when you follow your own wrong inclinations your lives will produce these evil results: impure thoughts, eagerness for lustful pleasure, idolatry, Spiritism (that is, encouraging the activity of demons) hatred and fighting, jealousy and anger, constant effort to get the best for yourself, complaints and criticisms, the feeling that everyone else is wrong except those in your own little group – and there will be wrong doctrine, envy, murder, drunkenness, wild parties, and all that sort of thing. Let me tell you again as I have before, that anyone living that sort of life will not inherit the kingdom of God."

To say that we are free to exhibit these filthy character traits and to participate in these ungodly activities and still claim to be children of God is foolishness if not something much worse! But isn't the blood of Jesus powerful enough to cover the vilest of sin? Of course, it is! That's how the abuser and murderer of over 100 beautiful women before his execution, repented and came to Christ. Ted Bundy on death row in a Florida prison asked for Dr. James Dobson to minister to him. Ted repented and came to Christ.

Notice! REPENTED! Repent and turn away from the filth! I John 1:9 explains how to deal with our sin – confess it, admit it to God. He is faithful and just to forgive us and to cleanse us! Hallelujah!

Then I John goes on to explain to us how we can KNOW we belong to Father. I John 2: 3, tells us the way we can KNOW we are His – "If we keep His commandments." Vs. 6 says it this way, "If we say we are Christians, if we say we abide in Christ, then we ought to walk (live) like Christ walked (lived)."

Jesus showed us the difference between "saying" and "doing" in Matt. 7:21. " It is not everyone that SAYETH, "Lord, Lord,……but he that DOETH the will of my Father!" Jesus warned us to beware the false prophet, Matt. 7:15-17. He may SAY the right thing, but he DOES the wrong things. The fruit of their lives is evil. Vs. 20 You will know the tree by its FRUITS. What fruit does my life produce?

PRAYER: Father, my desire is to drop the old human nature, the nature that produces the evil fruit described in Gal 5:19-21. All those things are filthy, unhealthy, unwholesome. I want to be like you. II Pet. 1:4 says I can be a partaker of Your Divine Nature, escaping corruption! That is my desire. Teach me how, Father. Teach me to stand on the promises! To daily add to my life those good things You have for me – virtue and knowledge and self-control and perseverance. To turn my back on any deceiver that would tell me I can claim all Your blessings and live like the devil! Open my mind to Your truth. Open my heart to Your leading! Amen.

Day Thirteen

VS.4

REFUSING THE LORDSHIP OF CHRIST

"...ungodly men, turning the grace of our God into lasciviousness, and denying the only Lord God, and our Lord Jesus Christ."

It is so easy to celebrate our **SAVIOR**! We were deep in the pit of despair! We were drowning in the depths of sin, crying for someone to rescue us! "Then the Savior reached down for me. He had to reach way down for me!" (from the song) His hand grabbed us and brought us out! Hallelujah! We are saved! Safe in the arms of Jesus! The New Birth brings with it joy unspeakable and is full of glory! We have new desires, new insights, new goals, a new hope, a new future! Let's celebrate! Amen! Never, ever fail to celebrate that day, to rejoice at that marvelous rescue!

THEN, at some point after this life-changing experience of being saved, we are confronted with the need to accept Christ as

LORD! We are asked to consider Him in every decision, seek His approval before each choice. Whoa! Wait a minute! I'm my own boss! I can make my own decisions! No, you can't! Not if HE is Lord. As Lord, He is Master. As Lord, He calls the shots. As Lord, His will comes first!

Why do you think Jesus said, "If you will be my disciple, you must deny yourself and take up your cross and follow me." Why do you think Paul said, "I die daily." Self is very self-centered! What letter is in the center of S-I-N? Do you see it? At the center of S-I-N is "I". We all have "I" problems. Watch a toddler, playing with his playmates. You will hear a lot of "MY, MINE, ME, I." Humans have to be taught to share! It doesn't come naturally! We are naturally "I" centered.

To say that we can do as we please, that we are free to pleasure self, is to deny the Lordship of Christ. At the end of Christ's life and ministry, He admitted that He didn't want to die. He found no pleasure in suffering stripes for our healing. He was not laughing hanging on a cross nearly naked in front of Jerusalem, of bleeding out on Calvary's cross to save us. But after much prayer and submission of Himself to the Father, He said, "Never the less, not MY will, but THINE be done."

What if you fail to make Him Lord? What if you make wrong choices, go the wrong way? And, you probably will at some point. All of us have, somewhere in our Christian experience, failed to take into account God's will before making a decision. To carelessly or haphazardly make a mistake is not the same thing as to **choose to** make yourself Lord in your life, to put yourself on the throne of your life. The key to making Christ the Lord of your life is to step off the throne, repent (not just feeling sorry about, but also changing directions, turning around), learn from it and go on – make progress!

To give Jesus the Lordship of your life means you don't want to say anything you wouldn't say if you could see Jesus standing in your presence. You don't want to do anything you wouldn't want Jesus to see you do. You want your life to look like Jesus' life. You want your words to be like Jesus' words. For in fact, Jesus **is** present with you. He said, "I'll never leave you." To deny Him is to deny His authority over your life.

To deny Him is to deny that He is the creator of moral laws and the Chief Judge as to when those laws are broken. To say that there is good and evil in the world, infers that there is a standard by which we judge what is good and what is evil. Who creates that standard? If we say mankind, then we are to expect the standard to be constantly changing. We know God is the same always, therefore His standard is a law that will never change. Let us acknowledge Him as Lord, as Master, as Judge!

PRAYER: Father, I worship You. You are Lord of the universe. Today, I make You Lord over my life, over my circumstances, over my choices, over my behavior. Yes, I realize that I will have to submit my will again tomorrow, that my old flesh nature likes to resurrect and come back to take over. But for today, and afterward, one day at a time, I choose to make you LORD! Jesus, be LORD in my life!

Day Fourteen

VS. 5

"LET ME REMIND YOU..."

Isn't it peculiar how we must often be reminded of lessons we once learned? Peter said in II Pet. 1:12, "I will not be negligent to put you always in remembrance of these things." In II Pet. 3:1 "...I stir up your pure minds by way of remembrance." We humans have the capability of putting things out of our minds. If we fail to see something as very important, or perhaps if it is a painful memory, we can just shove it to the back of our minds.

Jude is about to warn us of something very important, something very dangerous, something so threatening that he gives not just one example, but three examples to illustrate the truth and to clarify the understanding of a Bible truth.

Example one is given in Vs. 5 of Jude; Example two is named in Vs. 6; Example three is detailed in Vs. 7. Before we try to understand the examples, let's consider the nature of God expressed in Exodus 34:6-7. God is explaining His nature to Moses. God says to Moses, I AM "merciful and gracious, long-suffering and abundant in goodness and truth, keeping mercy for thousands, forgiving iniquity and transgression and sin...." Yes! That is OUR God, OUR Father, OUR everlasting Tower of Strength. He cares for us. He accepts us. He forgives us. Yes, this is the nature of our God!

Keep reading. The next word is AND! There is another side to His nature. And it is just as much God as the above description. The scripture continues, "And that will by no means clear the guilty..." Just because God loves us and just because He is merciful and forgiving, that does not mean He will excuse sin. That's why Jesus had to come and die!

In thinking back to our own childhoods and the memory of our earthly fathers, we remember those times of his tenderness, those times of his rescuing us. We remember our pride in his strength as he defended us from our enemies. Then, on the other hand, we also remember those times where he corrected us, when the strength of his arms was used to spank us. God, our Heavenly Father, is also strong in correcting His beloved children. The love of God does not automatically erase our sin. Our sin must be dealt with. There is still a penalty for sin.

That's why Jesus came - to seek and to save that which was lost. He died, shed His blood to wash our sin. Does that mean that ALL will be saved? Automatically? No, Rom. 10:9-10 tells us we have a part – 1. Believe the plan of God and 2. Accept the plan for yourself, and 3. Confess your faith in and acceptance of God's plan. Acts 2:21 and Romans 10:13 quotes Joel 2:32 saying "whosoever shall call upon the name of the Lord shall be saved." Something for you to do.

Our God is a just God, a God whose love and mercy does not automatically clear the guilty. That's why Jesus came – because God's nature also requires justice for wrongdoing. Who gets to decide what is right and what is wrong? God does. His is the great yardstick by which we measure what is true, His law is the moral ruler, His way is the right way. How, then, can mere mortals ever measure up? Through Jesus!

Not only does Jesus pay our debt, settle our score with Father, erase the list of mess-ups we have acquired, but He also comes inside us to enable us, empower us to live pleasing to Father. Now just think how disappointing it will be to God, if after all His provision, after all His preparation, we refuse to use the resources He provides and refuse to follow His plan in our daily lives. Jude says that is denying the Lordship of Jesus Christ. Jesus told us what happens if we deny Him in this earth! Matt. 10:33.

PRAYER: Heavenly Father, thank you for providing the sacrifice for our sin, the Blessed Jesus. Thank you for giving us minds to believe the truth. Thank you for providing the message of truth, both in the scripture and through people. Father, please help us do our part – to believe, to receive and to call on your name. Come and live in me, that I might be an example to others, an example that will lead them to the truth! Amen.

Day Fifteen

VS. 5

EXAMPLE ONE

Examples are pictures that are intended to clarify, to help us understand something better. A picture is not the real thing, it is a portrayal of part of the real thing. It is not usually three dimensional. It does not usually include the senses of smell or touch or taste, but it does help us visualize the real thing better than just words.

In example one, Jude brings us the picture of Israel being delivered from slavery in Egypt. Israel, God's chosen people, found themselves in bondage, obeying the Pharaoh, working for his benefit, not able to decide for themselves where they would live or what they would do. When the mistreatment became severe, the Pharaoh murdering their babies, beatings and privations by Egyptian soldiers, the Israelites began to pray to their God, asking for deliverance.

The scriptures list no superior qualities that would encourage God to deliver Israel from their oppressors. The only characteristic mentioned is that they were the seed of Abraham. God had made a covenant, a legal contract, with Abraham that God would bless those that blessed Abraham and his seed, that God would curse those who cursed Abraham and his seed. God never forgets His part of the covenant! He sent Moses and delivered the people out of their affliction, out of their bondage and out of their misery.

The children of Israel are out of Egypt! They are free! No longer do they work for the Pharaoh's benefit! No task master stands over them with a whip! Their children have a chance to grow up free! They are God's people!

Moses learned an amazing truth! **It is much easier to get the people out of Egypt, than it is to get Egypt out of the people!** God shows Himself strong in their behalf, over and over. He feeds them with manna from Heaven. He opens the Red Sea for them to escape, walking across on dry land. God sends water for them to drink - in the desert - from a rock! They grumble that they have no meat and He sends quail flying at arm's length so that they can just reach up and pluck them from the sky. Their clothes and shoes do not wear out or become too small. God heals them from snake bites, puts a cloud over them to cool them in the daytime and a pillow of fire to warm them at night. All this, yet they still long for the leaks and onions of Egypt!

God loves them, provides for them, protects them. That's His grace. Do they deserve it? No. They grumble and gripe when something does not please them. They rebel against the leadership God provides. God leads them with a cloud by day, a pillow of fire by night. Look at the grace of God! Still they yearn for the leeks and onions of Egypt.

Then the pronouncement is made. No one above the age of forty will enter the promised land. But wait! There is an exception! Joshua and Caleb, the two faithful spies who BELIEVED! They will enter! Other than those two, the entire company, all of which had experienced the mercy and grace of God, would die in the wilderness. Note how the King James Version states it. "the Lord, having saved the people....afterward destroyed them..."

What caused this "afterward destroyed them"? If you have followed this story you could see it coming! Moses pleads with God several times for the people, when it was God's choice to destroy them. Does this mean our God is capricious? That He is easily ticked off? That we must step lightly around Him least we upset Him? No, but as an example to us, God brought judgment. We must know, we must never forget, that God is a God of great mercy, **and** that He is a God of justice and justice requires judgment on the disobedient.

PRAYER: Dear Father, help me never forget, that You are bounteous in mercy! Your grace is beyond anything we have ever experienced on this earth, yet, You have warned us that Your children have standards that make them the royalty of this creation! You have explained those standards in Your Word, but You do more than inform! You also empower us to live up to those standards by Your Spirit coming inside us, giving us POWER to say NO to wrong and to choose the right! When we don't believe You, when we deliberately refuse to follow Your plan, You will let destruction come. Father, forgive my shortcomings and continue to "strive" (Genesis 6:3) with me.

Day Sixteen

JUDE, VS. 6

EXAMPLE TWO

In II Peter, Chapter 2, Apostle Peter is sounding a warning to the saints, concerning false prophets and false teachers. It sounds very similar to Jude's warning. Peter tells three examples of God's willingness to bring judgment on the same creation He once blessed. His first example was the angelic beings who left God's plan for them. He then lists what he calls the Old World, the world before Noah's flood. Then finally he recalls the cities of Sodom and Gomorrah.

Jude uses some of the same language in Jude verse 6 to instruct us. "The angels which kept not their first estate, but left their own habitation..." The angels, Jude says, speaking of the one-third of Heaven's angels which followed Lucifer, "kept not their first estate." God had a plan for them, a purpose for them, a place for them, but they refused to hold on to it, to contend for it, to endure. And what was the result? Judgement! Destruction!

Beloved, you, too, will be tempted to turn loose of the gifts which God places in your life. It is easy to let go of the holiness that God brings to us when He pulls us out of the pit, washes us in His blood, cleanses us from sin and sets our feet on the new highway. The enemy will whisper, "This way is too hard. Choose the easier pathway." Or he will tell you to forget the peace God gives, with "You are not having any fun. Look at the fun your friends are having on the broad way..." Yeah – that path leads to destruction! Be reminded of Moses' choice. He chose to bear the hardships with the people of God rather than to enjoy the "pleasures of sin for a season." Heb. 11:25.

To determine which path is the wiser, look at the end of it! Where is this path going? Remember there is a way that seems right to man, but the end thereof is death. Prov. 14:12. Is the "season of pleasure" worth the end result?

Isn't it peculiar how *getting* is always more fun than *keeping*?! The *getting* is "new", exciting, different! The *keeping* is often tedious, labor intensive, same ole', same ole'. But to Keep God's First Estate is to value, treasure, hold on to what God gives, what God plans for us. To see the wisdom of and the good in God's plan will motivate us to be determined to "Keep it!"

Not only did those fallen angels refuse to contend for, to keep, those good things God put in their lives, but also Jude says, "they LEFT their own habitation..." They walked away from the dwelling place God had assigned them. They Left. That reminds me of the instruction, "Here is the good path. Walk in it." Isa. 30:21. But human tendency is to say, "Oh, no. We want to go our own way, thank you very much. We will walk where we please."

These angels were once servants of the most High. At one time they, too, worshipped around the throne. They were ambassadors, representatives of Holy God. Did anyone force them from the presence of God? Did something snatch them from God's hand? No, the verse says, "they left..."

We, too, can choose. God gives us free will. We can choose to follow God, or follow God's enemy, the devil. Let us not be deceived into thinking that if we follow God's enemy we can claim God's blessings. No, if we align ourselves with God's enemies, we will also be destroyed with His enemies.

Seeing God's provision on this earth, the variety, the beauty, the functionality, the abundance, we can only begin to imagine God's Heavenly habitation which He had prepared for the angels. Yet, they chose to leave.

If we choose to leave what God is preparing for us, we are even more foolish than the angels, for we have the interest of our inheritance, the down-payment on the total, a little taste of Heaven to go to heaven in, the Holy Spirit's presence in our lives here on earth. A warning here! God will not throw you out of the path of the righteous, but you can choose to LEAVE. No devil of hell is big enough to pull you out of the family, but you can choose to leave! And the final warning is this! SINCE GOD DID NOT SPARE THOSE ANGELS, HE WILL NOT SPARE YOU. IF YOU MAKE THE SAME CHOICE, YOU TOO WILL MEET JUDGMENT & DESTRUCTION!

PRAYER: Oh, Father. My heart grieves with Yours at those who have made the choice not to hold fast to the GIFT You have given us, for those who have chosen not to STAY on the Heavenly Highway. Please help us listen to Your caution to those who LEFT THEIR FIRST LOVE, to repent! Thank you for that door You hold open – REPENTENCE. Another chance! REPENT! O, Lord. I repent now, for like Isaiah said, "I am a man of unclean lips and I dwell in the midst of a people of unclean lips." (Isa.6:5) Dear Lord, do to us now, even as You did for Isaiah, take a coal off the Heavenly altar and cleanse us, cleanse our talking, cleanse our thinking, cleanse our doing. Thank You, Father. Amen.

Day Seventeen

JUDE, VS. 7

EXAMPLE THREE

Though all three example groups suffered destruction and judgment, there were differing reasons. The first example states the people brought destruction on themselves because <u>they believed not</u>. They didn't believe God's promises of a better place. They refused to take God's warnings seriously. They refused to obey.

The second group, the angels, just <u>left their place</u> with God. We need to take heed, that we not deliberately walk away from God, His calling and purpose for our lives, His will for us. No devil of hell is able to take us out of the Father's hands, but Father will allow us to exercise our free will, which He gave us, to walk out of His hands, to leave.

The third example group <u>gave themselves over to sexual immorality and homosexuality</u>. It was a deliberate choice. They GAVE themselves over to these unnatural expressions of the beautiful expression of married love God gave us. These beautiful temples, our bodies, God made for a specific purpose. This third example group refused to submit to God's purpose. Instead, they gave their bodies over to impurity and self-centered pleasure.

Some groups teach that the original sin was when Adam and Eve had sex in the garden, that all sex is sinful. Anyone who knows the scriptures knows better than that.

God is the creator of sex and said all He created was very good. (Gen. 1:31). In fact in Gen. 1:28 God commanded the man and woman to be fruitful and multiply. What a generous God! He could have spoken every human into existence! Instead, He allowed humans to play a part in creating life! And said it was very good!

In fact this gift of creating life and enjoying the connectedness of becoming one is so very precious that God protects it with laws, prohibitions, and restrictions so that the very act is elevated and reserved for the covenant relationship called marriage. And marriage, God's way, is understood to be a covenant between a man and woman. God Himself made this decision in the beginning, saying, "Therefore shall a man leave his father and his mother, and shall cleave to his wife: and they shall be one flesh." Gen.2:24.

This vile group who refused to honor God's way, were destroyed with eternal fire. What is God's way described here in Genesis that the third example group refused? First is a "leaving" of father and mother, the birth unit, to create a new family. "Leaving" or separating emotionally, spatially, financially is often tearing, but it is necessary. We must establish a new unit of family, a new relationship, new authority figures, new chains of command. God shows us how – "leave."

The second step in establishing God's plan for the family is to "cleave" to one another. This word shows a determined clinging, a decision to stay together, regardless. I am sometimes amused when a young wife tells me, "I don't love him anymore!" Honey, feelings will come and go, but love is a decision. Just DECIDE to treat your spouse right! Just hang in there! The feelings of romance will come back if you are determined to treat the loved one with affection and respect. Put forth the effort to "cleave!" God gives exceptions to this rule. One exception is when there is physical abuse of spouse or children. Another is when the spouse walks out and abandons his responsibilities in the relationship. Other than those two exceptions, we are commanded to 'CLEAVE!" Stick together!

The third step is "become." Becoming shows a progressive work. It is not accomplished in one day. In fact, marriage is a life time work! Couples have multiple areas in which they are "becoming" one. In physical intimacy, yes, we are learning to pleasure our mates, but there are other areas, such as the handling of our finances, the rearing of children, spiritual growth, work, relationships with friends, family, and neighbors. All these areas take struggling to become like-minded, in agreement!

When we deliberately choose to leave God's plan for sex and the family, we find ourselves getting into all kinds of filthy expressions of our God-given gift of sexuality, trying so hard to find fulfillment and pleasure. When you follow God's plan, you will find such joy in just admitting that God had a good plan, and that He wants you to enjoy one another.

Then Jude mentions the sexual sin of "strange flesh." Homosexuality is called an abomination to God, "strange" or abnormal. It seems to be the ultimate in rebellion against God. "I don't like who God made me, so I will make myself someone different." We must never accept this "strange" expression as normal, but lovingly point to God's way. There is abundant love, great joy and great peace found in following God's way!

PRAYER: Father, I may not always be totally successful at following your plan for my life, at reflecting Your way to those around me, but it is my desire to do so. Please, empower me with Your Spirit to walk like You, to talk like You, to fulfill Your calling for me. Thank You for Your strength, Your power, Your Spirit which You so generously share with humans. Amen.

Day Eighteen

JUDE, VS. 8

BEWARE FILTHY DREAMERS WHO DEFILE THE FLESH

Remember how in vs. four, Jude grieves that "ungodly men" have crept in among us, and many of the saints are unaware of the danger these men bring with their spurious teaching. Well, in verse 8, Jude calls these same men "filthy dreamers" and lists three sins they practice unashamedly.

A dreamer is one who is not totally in touch with reality. He is asleep. He is not aware of dangers present. Our adversary, the devil, loves to catch us unaware. Our being asleep makes it easier for him to steal, kill and destroy. It is often deadly for us to fall asleep on our watch. Jesus said, "Watch and pray, that ye enter not into temptation." Matt. 26:41.

One sin Jude states these ungodly men do is "defile the flesh." Since Jude says it is possible to sully, mar or spoil this flesh, I'm going to define this "flesh" as the body, not the carnal mind often called "the flesh" in Scripture.

This body God placed you in is precious. It is the only house you will have to live in here on this earth. The only way you have to move out of this house is to die. Therefore, shouldn't we take good care of this house? To defile is to mar, sully or spoil. Of course there are sexual sins which defile our flesh, but there may be others. I will express a few and you give prayerful thought as the Lord may bring to your mind ways you are being careless with your house.

Body piercings and tattoos may come to mind as you consider how one might mar, sully or spoil "the flesh." Thank God, all sin is forgivable except that one Jesus talked about. If you have engaged in the previously mentioned marring of your house, forgive yourself, ask God for forgiveness and move on. Since Jude is talking to the Body of Believers, he may be thinking of ways we in the Family sometimes mar, sully or spoil our bodies. One way is lack of rest. God gave man a Sabbath, a day of rest. To keep our bodies in good shape we need that day of rest. If you are in ministry, you work on Sunday, but you could set aside another day, or two half days, to spend with your family and to rest from your labors.

To keep our bodies in good shape, we need certain nutrients usually provided by our food. If you find you are not getting enough of some nutrient, you can take supplements. To keep our bodies in good shape, we need exercise. Many modern jobs require hours of sitting. Our bodies are made to move. Hours of sitting causes loss in the muscles, joints, in the bones and in the organs. We must discipline ourselves to walk or go to the gym to keep our houses in good shape.

I was reared by two holiness preachers. I thank God for my parents. Because they lived clean lives, I have inherited few weaknesses in my body. But one negative was that "everything" was a sin. We couldn't play ball, because the teams might play on Sunday or the uniforms were not appropriate for girls! We couldn't play in the band because the girls, as well as the boys, wore slacks. We couldn't go to the gym because exercise dress was not "Godly!"

But we could EAT! So guess what we did! Every celebration, every fun time was centered around eating.

I know this is a sensitive area. I am not pointing fingers or accusing anyone of gluttony. I know there are medical reasons some bodies do not process food well, extracting the nutrients needed to provide energy for life. But it would be dishonest not to consider before God, "Am I abusing my body with food?"

My weakness is ice cream. I can eat ice cream anytime of the day or night! I can eat ice cream on a full stomach! I can eat ice cream in cold weather. If given enough time, I feel sure I can find a scripture somewhere that declares there is ice cream at the Marriage Supper of the Lamb! I can easily abuse my body with ice cream and not even feel guilty, but blessed! To be disciplined in eating, to be temperate, to be controlled, to keep my body in good shape takes great resolve. God help me!

PRAYER: Dear Father, I want to please You in every area of my life. Please help me to take care of this house You gave me. Give me the resolve, the determination, the discipline to say "no" to the pleasures that are defiling to the flesh. Amen.

Day Nineteen

VS. 8, 2ND SIN

DESPISE DOMINION

Look up the definition of "dominion." You will probably be surprised. You may find as I did, that your carnal mind does some "despising dominion!" Dominion is sovereignty; control. Synonyms are dominance, authority, mastery, control. All of us can recall some time when we resented the authority or dominance someone had over us. In fact the subject of submission to authority has much space in the Scriptures.

You men probably think only the females in the audience have problems with despising dominion, but notice Eph. 5:21, where Paul is giving three keys for staying FULL of the Spirit. The third is "Submitting yourselves one to another." Submitting is not just an action, a giving in of one's own will, but it is also an attitude, willingness to say, "I honor your position, your place of dominance in my life."

When I had a bit of a problem discussing this topic, the Holy Spirit said to me, "Do you think your reluctance to write on this topic may reveal that you are having a problem living out this principle of submission?" Who me? Yes, me. I do. You do. Every human does. Several months ago my husband questioned some statement, some decision I had made. My retort, "Well, God gave me a brain, and it works!" Yes, that's true. God gave each of us a mind, a will, emotions. That's known as soul. Yet, it is sin to desire pre-eminence, control, in positions God has not placed us.

Look at Philippians 2:3-10. In simple language, (Janell's paraphrase!), "Do nothing to lift yourself up but lift up someone else. Be just as concerned about the problems and needs of others as about your own. That is what Jesus did! Though He was God, He did not insist on His rights as God, but deliberately took the position of servant (human) stooping to die for man's sins, even the criminal's death on a cross. Because of this God the Father, lifted him up, exalted him and gave him a name above every name, that at that precious name of Jesus every knee, and I mean EVERY knee, EVERY KNEE EVERY WHERE, shall bow." Hallelujah! God lifted Jesus up! Let God do it, Friend! Let God lift you up!

We humans, especially we humans in America, have difficulty giving up our rights! "But this is our God-given right!" OK, if God put us in that position, then we should stand our ground, but if our human pride is wanting preeminence, then it is our God-given responsibility to bring self under control and deliberately put our foot on our pride, submit to God's will and to the authority God has put over us. Is it in the home? Is the control you resent in the church? Maybe it is in your work? God has order. There is a chain of command. Let's find our place and refuse to sin by despising dominion.

In many of the churches "we" pastored, I was Praise and Worship leader. During some services, I would get "anointed" or at least feel I was, and get lost in the songs of worship that were so dear to my heart. Sometimes, Pastor would stand to take the service before I was ready to come down off my high. My soulish self would feel, "Just a few more minutes, please. We are about to hit pay dirt! The Spirit is high! Let's sing that chorus one more time!" One of the things I had to learn was that God had put Pastor in charge of the service. If he felt it was time to go on with the service, I had no authority to continue with my part. "But, Lord," I rebutted, "I feel You here and people are being blessed!" The Spirit replied to my heart, "If Pastor misses My leading, he'll get the spanking; but if you rebel, you'll get the spanking!" Oh, wow! Was I ever ready to put that service back into the proper hands!

PRAYER: Dear Father, Thank you for Your patience with us as we learn to do things Your way. You know our frame, that we are often weak and tempted to take charge when it is not our place to take charge. Please let us rest in Your will, rest in Your way, rest in Your plan, trusting You to make every situation work out right. It is such a relief to know that our future doesn't depend solely on our actions and decisions. We have a great big wonderful Father who holds us in the palm of His hand and when it seems someone is just going to run over us, if we don't assert ourselves, we can put everything back in Your hand and trust You to handle it, especially if that someone is our God-given authority! Thank you for helping us discern Your way, Your authorities, Your will for our lives. Amen.

Day Twenty

VS. 8, 3ᴿᴰ SIN

SPEAK EVIL OF DIGNITIES

You know how, as you study the Bible, day after day, the Lord will give you different understandings of the same verse of scripture. Today's understanding will meet the need of today, will match the level of maturity and understanding of today, will answer the question you are struggling with today. That's how the same scripture can be milk for the babe, bread for the child, and meat for the mature saint.

This word dignities, ("doxa" in the original language) in the N.T. always represents a positive - praise, honor, glory, an appearance commanding respect, magnificence, excellence. Jude went on to say, (Janell's paraphrase of vs. 9) Look how carefully the arch angel, Michael, spoke to even the devil, when contending over Moses' body. He refused to pronounce a reviling judgement of him (the devil), but said instead, "The Lord rebuke you."

If we should be that careful when speaking about, or to the decidedly wicked one, the enemy of the saints, how much more careful ought we to be when talking about, or to any of our brothers and sisters in the family of God.

How much better off would the church be, if we refused to speak negatively of our brothers and sisters in Christ! Will you always agree with every Christian you know? Of course not! Will everyone always please you? Of course not! Just remember what James said of that little member, the tongue! "Behold, how great a matter a little fire kindleth! And the tongue is a fire...." James 3:5-6.

These evil dreamers in Jude did not have their tongues under control, but used them to speak evil of people and things when they had no clear understanding or knowledge of the facts. (Jude vs. 10). Even if you KNOW something to be the truth, it is better left unsaid if it will hurt one of God's "little ones" or damage the cause of Christ.

Years ago, the PCG Bishop, Dr. R. Dennis Heard, preached a message he entitled, "When It Is Wrong to tell the Truth." I know, I was stunned, too, when he announced his topic. Then he started his dissertation with these words, "It is never right to tell a lie, but sometimes it is wrong to tell the truth." Then he proceeded to show his audience, that many times we would be far better off to keep our mouths shut and refuse to say anything, rather than hurt a little one or the cause of Christ.

Learn a trick of communication from Christ! When He didn't want to answer a question, he responded with a question! The chief priests and leaders of the temple came to Jesus and asked, "Who gave you the authority to do these things?" (Clean up the temple?) Jesus responded, "Let me ask you a question and if you answer it, I'll answer yours. The baptism of John, was it from God or of men?" Those leaders knew they were in trouble, no matter how they answered! Matt.21:23-27.

Speaking negatively and judgmentally of anyone is unnecessary unless you have been called as a witness before a council, or unless God has directed you to warn the family of God of an evil doer, parading among the sheep, a wolf in sheep's clothing. I remember the elders saying, "Unless you can say something good about them, say nothing at all!"

PRAYER: Dear Father, please help me keep my tongue under the control of the Holy Spirit. The Word says, "The person who does not offend in word, the same is perfect." (James 3:2). Lord, I haven't made it to perfection! But I have a great desire to please You, both in this area of using the tongue and in presenting my body a living sacrifice. Please forgive me those times when I have hurt Your cause with my mouth.

Day Twenty-One
JUDE, VS. 11
WARNING, 3 SINS

"Woe unto them!" For they have 1. Followed in the footsteps of Cain, 2. Like Balaam, taught people to sin, and got paid for it, and 3.Like Korah, opposed the leaders God chose, in this instance, Moses.

Today's warning is don't follow in the footsteps of Cain. Jesus taught us that murder starts in the inner man, often as anger. Matt. 5:21-22. In Genesis 4 where the story of Cain is told, the two sons of Adam and Eve have brought offerings to God. The Bible states how Abel brought the best of his lambs. Cain just brought a gift of his crops. Then he became angry because his gift was not accepted. God confronts him over his anger and encourages him about the future, saying, "You will be accepted, if you do what is right." Gen.4:6-7.

Have you ever found yourself angry because someone, whom you have judged as not as good as you, has received a blessing? One of the things we must remind ourselves is that man often judges from outward appearances while God looks at the heart. I Sam. 16:7. I once learned a good lesson about God's judgement and mine!

I was having some difficulties with my knees. I was about 50 years old and the old knees did not want to lift this body up to the next step, especially with the box of books I was carrying to the Ladies meeting!

Pastor Richter, always invited the young ministers in our congregation to the front of the auditorium to pray for those who needed "anointing" and "laying on of hands" during the Sunday morning service. If a guest minister was visiting, Pastor often invited them to join our student ministers in ministering to the people. I was playing the organ while the prayer service was going on and the Spirit spoke to my heart, "Go let Bro. _____," a guest minister visiting with us that morning, "pray for you and I'll heal your knees."

There was a problem in my heart. Bro. _____, the visiting minister, had just been relieved of his credentials for taking a woman, not his wife, to a local motel for the night! "Lord, I don't have any confidence in his prayers. I know all these young preachers. I have confidence in them!"

"Do you want your knees healed?" the Holy Spirit spoke to my heart. I motioned to the other musicians to keep playing, and climbing off the organ stool, went and stood in front of the guest minister. I closed my eyes and bowed my head. It seemed like several minutes, but the minister had not yet touched my head. I looked up at him, amazed! Tears were streaming down his face, wetting his shirt and tie! "See," the Lord said to me, "he's repented and I've forgiven him, but you haven't!" The man laid his hand on my head and the Lord healed me! I have had no problems or pain with my knees since! But the greatest thing is the lesson I learned. God knows the heart! We often don't!

Anger or resentment over someone else's blessing, may not lead you to murder, but it will hinder you from receiving God's best. We are to rejoice with our brothers and sisters when they rejoice! Weep with them when they weep. Let's not follow in Cain's shoes, but seek to please God with all our deeds. Whatever we do, do it as to the Lord.

PRAYER: Father, thank you for your wonderful ways and the truths you reveal to us. You have taught us not to even compare our gifts, but to just give our best. And if we bring our gift and remember that we have something in our hearts against our Brother or Sister, to leave it there and go be reconciled with our Brother. Thank you, Lord, for Your precious indwelling Spirit that is helping us to become more like You.

Day Twenty-Two

BALAAM TAUGHT PEOPLE TO SIN

JUDE VS. 11

Jesus warned us against causing anyone to stumble, fall, sin. I would certainly wonder what is the motivation for such a deed? Well, Jude reveals Balaam's motivation – money! The King, Balak, offered Balaam money to curse the Israelites. Balaam couldn't! God wouldn't let him! So Balaam offered King Balak an alternative!

"I'll teach you how to get their God to curse them!" he told the king! "Just let your most attractive women parade in front of their men in fetching apparel! That ought to do the trick!" Num. 31:16.

Human nature hasn't changed much over the centuries, has it? Why did God make men so visual? Why did He make females so attractive to men? Have you ever considered how that in the animal kingdom, the male of the species is most often the most attractive, the more decorated, the brightest colors of the animals. It is the male lion that has the mane; in birds, the male is always the brightest colors; the male deer has the antlers. In humans, however, it is the female that has the additions – the protruding breasts, shapely hips, the rounded rump!

God is purposeful in all He is and does. And since we know it is God's nature to bless, to do good, to enhance our lives, let's look for the way we can fit into God's plan; how we, too, can bless, do good, up-lift.

Ladies, since we recognize that God made men visual, admiring of God's design of the female body, let's not dress in a provocative way, to deliberately attract the men's attention to our bodies. Remember, "do all as unto the Lord!" Col. 3:23. May everything we do, even in how we dress, honor the intent of God, rather than draw attention to ourselves. I know, we can be excessive in everything, even our modesty, but let's seek to please God, rather than fit into the mold of this world.

How do we accomplish that? We can ask ourselves, "Is this outfit to draw attention to me, or does it allow me to bring glory to God?" Remember Balaam's purpose was to cause the men of Israel to sin, to entice them into immorality with the local women.

Will our appearance cause men to lust? Again, we recognize that we have no control over others' thoughts. We can, however, do our best to bring glory to the Lord, and not to bring attention to our bodies. A sweet Christ-like Spirit is always admirable. I Peter 3:3-4.

Have you considered how we sometimes spend much more time preparing our bodies to go to church than we spend in preparing our hearts, minds and spirits to go to the services. I know, man judges from the outward appearance, but God judges the heart! Women, in particular, want to look attractive! But, if we will prepare our attitude to meet with the Family. If the fruit of the Spirit, love, joy and peace, (Gal. 5:22) are evident in all our behavior, we will represent Christ well.

PRAYER: Father, our greatest desire is to honor you, to please you, to bring glory to you. Please help us to be wise in our behavior and in our choices, that we not lead anyone into sin. Amen.

Day Twenty-Three
JUDE, VS. 11
"SIN OF KORAH" NUM. 16

What was the sin of Korah? If you have taken the time to read Numbers 16, you will see that Korah says to Moses, "Why do you think you should be the leader? Aren't we all chosen of God? Aren't we all equal?"

Well, there is some truth in his reasoning! Remember, how can anything look deceptive if there isn't some truth to make the deception look real? So how do we recognize God's truth which will set us free? Yes, if we are born again, following Christ the best we know, seeking to be obedient to His will and Word, we are His children, loved by Him, protected by Him, provided for by Him, forgiven by Him! However, that does not make us all the same. Remember, Jesus' parable of the talents given to the three servants! One was given five talents, another two, and finally one. How were these talents distributed? – according to their abilities! Matt. 25:15.

Remember the listing of the Gifts of the Spirit Paul names in Romans 12 and I Cor. 12! Different gifts are given to different members of the Body as they are needed! Remember, if all were an "eye" where would the "hearing" be, etc. As members of the Body of Christ, it is wisdom to honor and respect each member of the Body and his/her gifting, as given by God, needed by the Body, in its proper place and time.

What pride it reflects to think we know better than God who should be the leader! Who should be given five talents! Who should be the "eye" or the "ear" of the Body! If you think God has gifted you in a certain way and the part of the Body (the church) you are in is not recognizing that, you have two choices. A) Move to another part of the Body (church) or B) Be patient until God's will is worked out in the situation where you are. One thing you DON'T want to do is revolt against God's choice of leadership and God's authority. Korah's judgement taught us that truth!

Jesus taught in Matt. 5 "Blessed are the meek (humble) for they shall inherit the earth!" In our culture, meekness is not considered a great attribute, but Jesus said it is. Meekness is recognizing who is the boss and submitting to that authority. The Boss may not always be right, but he/she is still the Boss. Submitting to authority is taught in God's Word.

In Ephesians 5:21, the Word says, "Submit to one another, out of reverence for Christ." What if you think the leader is wrong? Then go to his/her boss – the Lord is certainly all our boss. Tell Him all about it. He will right the wrong in His time and in His way. Remember if we elevate ourselves, God will humble us; but if we humble ourselves, God will exalt us. Let God do it, Beloved, especially if it is your husband or a church leader. Let us learn from Korah's example!

PRAYER: Dear Father, we are so thankful you have given us these examples in Your Word that we can learn Your way! Our human nature sometimes wants to stand up and be noticed. Help us to take on Jesus' divine nature and please You, submit to You, in all we say and do. Amen

Day Twenty-Four

JUDE, VS. 12-13

IDENTIFY DECEIVERS

We, in these last days, sometimes think our churches are the only ones who have problems. Jude warns the Christians of his day about those in the church that are deceivers and will cause problems. To help us identify these wolves in sheep's clothing, he gives six examples from nature. They are: 1) Like reefs in the sea, 2) Like shameless shepherds, caring only for themselves, 3) Like clouds blowing over the land, but giving no rain, 4) Like trees in autumn bearing no fruit, 5) Like wild waves of a stormy sea, 6) Like wandering stars out of their God-given courses.

Let's look at reefs in the sea. They are alive, made up of coral which grows and is often very colorful! Reefs are habitats for many sea creatures – BUT, since they grow, you can perhaps sail right over them this month, but run aground on the reef next month, with the hull of your ship, torn by the rough edges. Father, help us to be aware of those who look beautiful, but have rough edges that could destroy the Body.

2) Shepherds are needed, faithful workers among the sheep, BUT, when they have turned to caring mainly for themselves, they are dangerous to the flock. They rejoice in harvesting the wool, in profiting from the sale of meat, but are not faithful in protecting the little ones in the flock.

3) Clouds are a wonderful blessing. They shade us from the full force of the sun. They carry moisture from the oceans to the land, which is in deep need of rain. BUT, when clouds come without rain, they raise our hopes which are then unfulfilled. We look with joy and expectation for the great blessing of rain, and none comes.

4) At harvest time, usually in the Autumn, we look at our fruit trees, expecting fruit. We have our mouths set for tasty morsels of blessings, BUT the tree is baren. Not only is the disappointment hurtful, the fruit is necessary for our health! And isn't that the purpose of a fruit tree!? To bear fruit!

5) Waves of the sea in normal times are soothing, even refreshing to the sea itself, BUT when the waves are wild and the sea is stormy, the waves just toss up the yucky mire from the bottom, revealing the filth on the bottom of the sea. Then they are destructive to everything they strike!

6) Wandering stars, not staying in their God-given orbits. I don't know anything about stars not staying in their orbits, BUT I have seen humans not staying in their God-given callings and it is not a pretty scene. I have seen humans refusing to walk in God's paths, and they suffer from it.

Beloved, all of these strange things can happen in your church. Just be warned. Churches, remember, will have both the wheat and the tares! Remember the net cast into the sea – it may come up with both delicious fish and inedible trash! What is our part in these situations? Let the Holy Spirit do the separating! God has not placed us there to pull up the tares! That is His job! BUT DON'T FOLLOW AFTER THE DECEIVERS.

There will be disappointments, clouds without rain! KEEP YOUR EYES ON JESUS! FOLLOW HIM! YOU BE THE

ENCOURAGER! YOU BE THE EXAMPLE OF CHRIST-LIKE! YOU BE THE FRUIT-BEARER! YOU BE THE FAITHFUL SHEPHERD!

PRAYER: Father, thank You for Your warning, in the Word. Help us to stay so close to You, we will hear the sweet whisper of Your voice as You call us to follow You. Thank you, Faithful Shepherd, for protecting and providing for Your sheep. You are our all and all! Amen.

Day Twenty-Five

VS. 14-15

JUSTICE AND JUDGEMENT

Perhaps as a child in Sunday School you learned that Enoch and Elijah are two men who transitioned into Eternity without dying. That is about all we knew about Enoch. Here, in Jude, we learn that he also prophesied and that he had a vision of justice and judgement coming to this earth! Perhaps you, too, have wondered why the wicked get by with evil deeds. Throughout the scriptures you will find Godly men lamenting as to why the wicked are not punished for their deeds. Just wait! They will be!

Job, the book written to help us understand suffering in this world, laments in Job 21:7, that the wicked live long lives and are influential! David, in the Psalms, often reminds us that the wicked will get what's coming to them. Psalm 37:1 says, "Fret not thyself because of evildoers, neither be thou envious against the workers of iniquity. For they shall soon be cut down..."

Isa. 13:11 reads, "and I will punish the world for their evil, and the wicked for their iniquity..." Isa. 57:21 says, "There is no peace, saith my God, to the wicked!" Nahum 1:3 gives this insight, "The

Lord is slow to anger and great in power, and will not at all acquit the wicked."

Aren't we glad that our God is slow to anger, that He is merciful and kind? That He gives the wicked space to repent? At Abraham's time, God told Abraham that the inhabitants of the land had not yet filled their cup of iniquity to the full. He would give them time to repent, but eventually the land would go to Abraham's heirs. Abraham's family spent 400 years in Egypt while God gave the people of the Middle East 400 years to repent! God has given people of every age and place, time and space to repent. There will eventually be the justice and judgement spoken of in these verses of Jude.

Romans 14:10 speaks of the judgement seat of Christ. Hebrews 9:27 says, "It is appointed unto man once to die and after this the judgement." Jer. 23:5 foretells the Righteous Judge who shall "execute judgement and justice in the earth!"

Because we are children of God, God's enemy, Lucifer, hates us. We are often assaulted by his followers. But we can walk in peace, knowing our Father will care for us, that the victory over all the evil of this world is ours! Our Judge, Jesus, has already paid the debt for our sins and we are free from the guilt of sin, free from the bondage of Satan, we are free from the penalty of sin! "Jesus paid it all; all to Him I owe. Sin had left a crimson stain, but Jesus washed it white as snow!" (Song)

However, those who will not accept the payment Jesus paid for their sin, will still have judgement to endure. The Justice of God demands that all evil be atoned. That all sin and iniquity be paid. If you have not yet trusted Christ's payment with His own blood for the sin of the world, including yours, you will be judged guilty and not eligible for Eternal Life. Stop now and say, "Lord, I accept Your payment for my sin. Be Lord in my life. I will follow wherever You lead."

PRAYER: Father, thank you for your plan, the Sacrificial Lamb, who died for the sins of the world. Help us to show to those around us, that precious plan, that priceless gift – Your Amazing Love in Jesus, the Son.

Day Twenty-Six
VS. 16
MIS-USING WORDS

The judgement mentioned in Vs. 15 for all the "ungodly deeds" and "ungodly people" includes for ungodly speech! Throughout the Holy Bible we are warned that our words are important, that the tongue is powerful! In fact, Prov. 18:21 warns that "Death and life are in the power of the tongue!" Have you considered that humans are the only created creatures on earth given the power of speech? Let's study the power in our words.

There are four kinds of poor usage of words mentioned in this verse: murmuring, complaining, boasting, and flattering. There is a lot of talk in the Pentateuch about the "murmuring" of Israel as they journeyed from Egypt to the Promised Land. They complained about the food, they complained about the lack of water. As loving and patient as our Father God is, He got tired of it! Then one man, Korah, carried the complaining one step further! He complained about God's choice of leadership! "Tell all the people to move away from the tents of Korah and his cohorts," said God, "and I'll take care of this!" Then He caused the earth to open and swallow the complainers and all their families and stuff!

One day while our son, James, was home from Bible college, visiting, we all sat at the dinner table. The little girls began to complain about the meal. Son, James, jumped up and ran out the back door which was behind the table! "What are you doing?" ask one of the little sisters.

James peeked in the door, cautiously. He said, loudly, "I studied in the Bible where God let the earth open up and swallow a man who grumbled, and all his family! I didn't want to be too close, in case God decided to punish you girls for grumbling!" T h e r e weren't many grumbling words after that!

Let's judge that Murmuring and Complaining are just two types of grumbling and go on to the next misuse of words mentioned – Boasting. We can boast in the Lord; we can boast of the goodness of God as He works in the lives of His children, but these great swelling words mentioned in Vs. 16 are lifting up self! It is dangerous to even think more highly of ourselves than we ought to think, but when we use words to lift up self, we have entered a sphere of "pride" that will bring God's judgement on us. "Pride goes before destruction and a haughty spirit before a fall." Prov.16:18. Pride is refusing to accept the truth, that all we are and all we have is from our Father God. He is the giver of life and the giver of every good and perfect gift. Jesus put it this way, "Without Me, you can do nothing!" We have nothing in ourselves that we can contribute to help or bless others.

When the disciples returned to Jesus to report on their ministries, they said, "Even the demons were subject to us!" Jesus looked way in the past and said, "I saw Satan fall from Heaven!" Luke 10:17-18. Yes, we can rejoice when Jesus chooses to use us to bless the Body, but it is Jesus that did the blessing! In Acts 3 where Peter and John were used to heal the cripple, Peter responded to the crowd, "His name, through faith in His Name, hath made this man strong!" Since we are all cells in the Body of Christ, how can we boast that alone we have accomplished anything for Christ!

The last misuse of words mentioned here is "flattery to get something." Flattery is dishonest. If you express appreciation or admiration that is not sincere, you have lied. But to use words just to influence the object of your words to give you something you want, you have shown yourself to be self-centered, selfish, self-absorbed. Look at Eph. 4:29. "Let no corrupt communication proceed out of your mouth, but that which is good to the use of edifying, that it may minister grace unto the hearers." Whatever we say, let it be words that will build up, encourage, bless those who hear. Will they feel loved, accepted, supported by what we have said? "Be kind, tenderhearted, forgiving…!" Eph. 4:32. Let's ask Jesus to help us reveal Him in everything we do and say! Amen?

PRAYER: Father, we want to honor You and please You with our words. We want You to be proud of us. Help us to be so much like Christ that we, too, will be called "Christians!"

Day Twenty-Seven

VS. 17-19

REMEMBER WARNINGS

Reminders usually come from people who have more experience, more age, more wisdom, than we who are being reminded. Jude says remember what the Apostles of the Lord warned you, there will come into your presence people who will make fun and their main reason for doing so is that they are following fleshly desires.

Consider Romans 8:1. "There is therefore NOW no condemnation to them which are in Christ Jesus, who walk not after the flesh, but after the Spirit." If we are following Christ, being led of the Holy Spirit, we are NOT seeking to please the flesh; we are not seeking to fulfill fleshly desires. First of all, we are not carrying the guilt of sin. Jesus took that away! Hallelujah! We are not being ruled by sin, or addictions! Hallelujah! Jesus conquered that for us! We really don't care what the people of the world think about our devotion to Jesus! Our aim in life is not to please or impress the worldly crowd, but to please Jesus!

Think of this! If we are Children of the King, who do we need to impress! So what, if the people following the lusts of the flesh make fun of you! Their future is in one location and yours in another! They have no understanding of the Light and what it means to Walk in the Light! If we walk in the Light, we won't stumble into darkness. If we walk in the Light as He is in the Light we have fellowship with Him and all who are walking in the Light! I John 1:7. If we walk in the Light we can discern the Truth and will follow Truth!

How do we know we are walking in the Light? "He that loveth his brother, abideth in the light...BUT, he that hateth his brother is in darkness..." I John 2:10-11. If we have LOVE in us we have God in us for "God is Love." I John 4:8. Jesus said, "If you love me you will keep my commandments." The greatest commandment is to Love God with all that is in you and the second is to love your neighbor as yourself. If we have God in us, we will "walk", BEHAVE, like him!

You need not expect the World to admire you. They don't even recognize you! I John 3:1 . "What manner of love the Father hath bestowed upon us, that we should be called the sons of God: therefore the world knoweth us not, because it knew him not!"

Jude, Verse 19 identifies these scoffers by describing their behavior. <u>First,</u> they sow division. Division is a church problem Paul dealt with in First Corinthians. He described how we are each building blocks in the True Temple of God in today's world. "Know ye not, ye are the Temple of the Holy Ghost!" I Cor. 3:16. I Cor. 6:19. He also described us as the Body of Christ, each of us providing a part, a gift, a function. I Cor. 12:27. To be whole and complete, we have to work together, stick together, function together. Division destroys the power and the wholeness of the Body.

<u>Second</u>, they are sensual. That describes a human who is so tangled up in the natural man that all his desires, all his goals, all his efforts are concerned with human, natural functions. Some examples would be eating, sex, appearance. Have you ever thought of the truth that if you can see it, smell it, touch it, taste it, hear it, it is probably of this world and is passing away! It is not eternal. Eternal things

are rarely discerned by human senses! Eternal, Spiritual things are discerned by the Spirit!

<u>Third</u>, they have not the Spirit! How do we know? Rom.8:5, "For they that are after the flesh do mind the things of the flesh; but they that are after the Spirit the things of the Spirit." Vs. 14 "For as many as are led by the Spirit of God, they are the sons of God." If we have the Spirit of God we will seek after Godly things. We will spend our energies trying to walk like God, talk like God, love like God. Our behavior will be constantly imitating Jesus. That's why they were called "Christians" at Antioch, because they acted so much like our precious Jesus, the Christ!

PRAYER: Father, our greatest desire is to please You. Flood our being with Your Spirit so much that we act like You, talk like You, love like You. Fill us with Yourself, with Your Spirit. Let any who want to, laugh! We are happy to be Yours!

Day Twenty-Eight
VS. 20
BUILD UP

Most of the Book of Jude has been warnings, 1. "to stay faithful to the truth" and 2. "to beware of deception." But here in verse 20 (and it starts with the word "but") Jude issues a command "build up" yourselves. I'm reminded of the Old Testament scripture that says David encouraged himself in the Lord when he came back to Ziklag from battle and found the town destroyed, all the women and children kidnapped and all their valuables stolen. His fellow soldiers were so perturbed they talked about killing David, but David encouraged himself in the Lord. I Sam.30:6.

How do we do that? How do we "build up" ourselves, or encourage ourselves? We start with our "thought-life!" We must replace our negative thoughts with positive thoughts. We must refuse to feel hopeless and decide to put our trust in the Lord. We must quit recounting all our weaknesses and failures and start naming all our Heavenly Father's strengths and victories! We must remind ourselves that He is our Father and will take care of us!

There are hundreds of verses in the Bible that tell how God loves us, how He delights in showing His strength to rescue us, how He will deliver us from our enemies! When our enemy, the devil, wants to discourage you, remind yourself of the times in the past when Father saved you, delivered you, healed you, met your financial need, rescued you! As you remember past blessings, you will be encouraged that God will do it again!

Memorize Psalm 91! When we quote the verses we are reminded again and again of how God has saved His people. During the Viet Nam war, the American Bible Society handed out to servicemen New Testaments that exactly fit in the breast pocket of the fatigues worn at the time. A friend who trained at Fort Benning and attended our church while stationed there, returned safely from Viet Nam. He visited us again before going home. He was very excited to show us his New Testament with Psalms and Proverbs in the back. Shrapnel which he had encountered in a battle had pierced the Testament through till it got to Psalm 91 in the back of the testament. There the shrapnel stopped. When one flipped the pages of the New Testament, the torn path looked like a finger pointing to Psalm 91! God had shown Himself the deliverer!

Jude, in the New Living Translation states in Verse 20, "But you, dear friends, must build each other up…" How do we build each other up? Again, we divert the negative talk by recalling testimonies of God's deliverance, or remind each other of scriptures in which God promises to show His children grace and mercy. Give any testimony you remember of God helping anyone, then remind each other that God is no respecter of persons. What He has done for one, He is willing to do for you!

Another way we can build each other up is praying together. "Where any two agree as touching any one thing it shall be done of my Father…" Matt.18:19. "One can put a thousand to flight; Two can put ten thousand to flight." When we join in the prayer battle, the unity more than doubles our strength. They say one horse can pull a certain amount of weight, but two can pull more than double that amount of weight. I know it is true in prayer!

What about Jesus' statement, "Where two or three are gathered together in my name, there will I be in the midst of them!" Matt. 18:20. We know Jesus promised to never leave us nor forsake us, but we don't always feel Him, or recognize He is there. But, where two or three are gathered in His name, His presence is discernable! Have you noticed that even with just TWO, they won't both feel down or low at the same time!? One will lift the other up! God is Good!

Your mind is the battleground. Fill it with the Word! God's Word is truth and truth will make you free! John 8:32. Praying in the Spirit means different things to different faiths, but I can tell you praying in your prayer language is both refreshing and restful. You don't have to think what to say next, you just submit to the Spirit's utterance! Let's pray!

PRAYER: Dear Father, Thank You that You will always have someone nearby when we need to be built up in our faith and spirit. Thank You that Your Word encourages at every bump in the road of life, that You are there and we have nothing to fear. Thank You that Your children are encouragers. Thank You that the Holy Spirit is our constant Companion to remind us that You are faithful. You are our Comforter when everything around us looks dark and foreboding! You shine Your light on our path and help us to see our way home to You. Amen.

Day Twenty-Nine

VS. 21 & 22

SHOWING GOD'S LOVE AND MERCY

Our human nature, the nature we inherited from our natural parents, has a tendency to be concerned about SELF! When someone hurts us, our desire is to hurt them back! We use the term "get even!" But getting even often brings us lower on God's scale of righteousness! If that person has used sinful behavior to hurt us, then when we get even, we have brought ourselves down to their level! These two verses urge us to show God's love, God's mercy, rather than the desire to get vengeance. Doesn't the Word say, "Vengeance is mine, saith the Lord. I will repay!" Rom. 12:19.

Then how are we going to conquer evil in our world! Romans 12: 9-21 gives us the plan! God's way! "Be not overcome of evil; but overcome evil with good!"

We know that God's nature is love. "God is Love!" When we have God in our hearts, we have love in our hearts because God is love. Now, does that mean we will always feel affectionate toward someone we are striving to love? I have come to realize that love is a decision! A decision to treat someone right, even when you don't feel like it. Feelings of affection may come and go, but we can decide that we will treat even our enemies with mercy and forgiveness like Jesus did. As he hung on the cross, suffering from a severe beating, hair having been pulled out of his head and beard, thorns piercing his scalp, he said, "Father, forgive them…" Luke 23:34.

Showing God's love and mercy when we are being abused and refused is so unusual that it is a special witness to the world of the Love of God! Rom 12:14, "Bless them that persecute you!" Is it normal to bless someone who is persecuting you? Probably not! But it is Godly! It is a witness to the world that "greater is He that is in you than he that is in the world!" I John 4:4.

"If your enemies are hungry, feed them. If they are thirsty, give them something to drink. In doing this, you will heap burning coals of shame on their heads." Rom. 12:20. NLT. But what if you don't FEEL forgiving toward this person who hurt you? This scripture doesn't say anything about FEELING! It talks about DOING! I once asked the Lord to help me learn how to forgive. He reminded me how my Daddy built concrete steps. First he built a wooden form. Then he poured the concrete into the form. When the concrete had hardened and Dad took away the form, there appeared the permanent concrete steps.

When you want to forgive someone, you build a form with your actions, then God can pour in the forgiveness! Feed them, give them a gift, reach out to them. Your goodness toward them will probably bring shame (coals of fire!) that will cause them to think differently about the situation.

A pastor friend was teaching on this scripture in a small-group setting and he asked, "Have you ever put hot coals on someone's head?"

A woman shouted back, "No Pastor, but I have tried throwing hot water on him!"

That's not exactly what Jesus is saying! He says, Don't repay evil with evil. Do all you can to live at peace with everyone. You are not responsible for how others act. But do what YOU can to live at peace with those around you. Rom. 12:18. Let what YOU do, what YOU say, how YOU act, reflect the love and mercy of our Lord and Savior, Jesus.

Have you noticed in the gospels, especially in the KJV, how often it states, "Jesus was moved with compassion." That compassion, that mercy, motivated Jesus to do great miracles to meet desperate needs!

PRAYER: Dear Father, You know us, You know our weaknesses. You know how it is unlike us humans to be good to our enemies. Thank you for sending the Holy Spirit to enable us to be loving and forgiving when someone has mistreated us. If we do anything that is like You, it is because of Your indwelling Holy Spirit. Thank you for that power to help us in our desire to be more like You. Amen

Day Thirty
VS. 23
HATE THE SIN, LOVE THE SINNER

"Save with fear…hating even the garment spotted by the flesh….."

Defining "sin" as anything that is contrary to God's way, God's rules, God's truth, we can see how right it is to hate sin. God is love; God is order; God is beauty; God is righteous; God is everything good. In fact, James 1:17 says "Every good gift and every perfect gift is from above…" The Ten Commandments were given to help society live in peace and safety. These rules help us treat each other, as well as our possessions, with respect. Anyone can see how much more pleasant life is when everyone is treated with consideration and respect.

    Several months ago I went with friends to their rented storage space located in a large Public Rental unit on the south side of Atlanta, Ga. The Office was outside the security gate and since they needed to make contact with the office we pulled in to park. Reaching for the office door, we found it was locked! Right there in broad daylight on a busily travelled street, the office is locked! The worker opened the door, we went and took care of business, turned to leave, and found the door was locked! Again!

I said, "Son, when I was a child we didn't even lock our doors at night. We often slept with our heads lying on the window sill to get a breath of cool air!"

The young man said wistfully, "I wish I had lived at a place and time like that!"

I thought, "Yes, and I wish all American youths could experience the time when the whole community tried to live by the Bible and honesty and respect for all life was honored."

What has caused the desperately depraved life style that has become the usual here in our USA? Step One: The Ten Commandments were removed from public view and consideration. Step Two: Prayer and Bible Reading was removed from schools. Step Three: Innocent blood was shed - legally.

How can our children know what is right or wrong unless there is a standard by which we judge what is right or wrong? The Ten Commandments was that standard that our whole land, our entire nation used to judge between right and wrong.

When Bible and prayer was part of the public education system, everyone got to hear about God, even those whose parents did not go to church or consider God in their homes.

Finally, the sin of slaying innocent, helpless babies in abortion, opens the door for any vile treatment of anyone. The scriptures mention the "shedding of innocent blood" hundreds of times as being one of the sins God abhors specifically. Yet, we here in American have legally slain over 64 MILLION pre-born children!

When we consider even briefly these abhorrent behaviors that our culture has adopted, we began to wonder, "How can we love the sinner!?" Then we remind ourselves, "The old Deceiver is busy making those who are not surrendered to Jesus believe their only hope for having joy in this life is to satisfy the fleshly desires for fun, importance, sex, notoriety and more stuff!"

How we long to see our friends and family experience the peace, love and joy we find in trusting Jesus, obeying His Word, living in His truth! Not only do we have love, peace and joy in this life, but we know eternal life is our future inheritance! How exciting to have a little bit of heaven to go to heaven in!

Now, we can feel compassion for those who have not yet tasted the many good things God puts in the lives of His children! And if we can understand that Father wants ALL mankind to experience His never-ending, eternal and abundant love, then we know we MUST extend His invitation to everyone to COME "unto me ALL ye that labor and are heavy-laden and I will give you rest." Matt. 11:28. It is not His will that any should perish, but that all have eternal life. What stands in the way? Humans have a part to play! We must CHOOSE Him. We have that wonderful gift of CHOICE. He will not force His will or way on anyone. We must CHOOSE Him.

PRAYER: Oh, dear Father. How wonderful to be Your child! How much effort You have exerted to adopt us into Your family. Oh, how much You suffered to enable our deliverance from this sin cursed world and life-style! Now, I choose You, Your way, Your will, Your plan, Your future for me! Oh, thank You, thank You, thank You! I'm so excited to look into the future, a future filled with You and Your goodness! Amen.

Beloved Reader, if you need prayer or help in your effort to follow Christ, you can email me at caroljanellrichter@gmail.com.

May you find great joy in Him.

About the Author

Janell, a minister's wife for 58 years, has studied the Bible all her life. She is the mother of three children, graduate of Columbus University, founder of Evangel Temple Christian Academy, author of many Christian articles, writer of Sunday School literature, author of 3 books, Bible teacher and Jesus lover!